PRIMITIVE WORLDS

People Lost in Time

Prepared by the Special Publications Division
National Geographic Society, Washington, D. C.

PRIMITIVE WORLDS:
People Lost in Time

Published by
THE NATIONAL GEOGRAPHIC SOCIETY
MELVIN M. PAYNE, *President*
MELVILLE BELL GROSVENOR, *Editor-in-Chief*
GILBERT M. GROSVENOR, *Editor*
BART McDOWELL, *Consulting Editor*

Contributing Authors
NAPOLEON A. CHAGNON, NEVILLE DYSON-
   HUDSON, TOR EIGELAND, VICTOR ENGLEBERT,
   ELMAN R. SERVICE, E. RICHARD SORENSON,
   WILSON WHEATCROFT

Prepared by
THE SPECIAL PUBLICATIONS DIVISION
ROBERT L. BREEDEN, *Editor*
DONALD J. CRUMP, *Associate Editor*
PHILIP B. SILCOTT, *Senior Editor*
MARY ANN HARRELL, *Managing Editor*
JANE R. McCAULEY, ANN CROUCH RESH,
   NATALIE S. RIFKIN, *Research*

Illustrations
DAVID R. BRIDGE, *Picture Editor*
MARGARET CARTER, MARGERY G. DUNN,
   RONALD M. FISHER, MARGARET M.
   JOHNSON, MICHAEL W. ROBBINS,
   ELIZABETH C. WAGNER, *Picture Legends*

Design and Art Direction
JOSEPH A. TANEY, *Art Director*
JOSEPHINE B. BOLT, *Associate Art Director*
URSULA PERRIN, *Design Assistant*
JOHN D. GARST, JR., MARGARET A. DEANE,
   NANCY SCHWEICKART, ISKANDAR BADAY, *Map
   Research, Design, and Production*

Production and Printing
ROBERT W. MESSER, *Production Manager*
GEORGE V. WHITE, *Assistant Production Manager*
MARGARET MURIN SKEKEL, RAJA D. MURSHED,
   Production Assistants
JANE H. BUXTON, MARTA ISABEL COONS,
   CAROL A. ENQUIST, SUZANNE J. JACOBSON,
   PENELOPE A. LOEFFLER, JOAN PERRY,
   MARILYN L. WILBUR, *Staff Assistants*
MARTHA K. HIGHTOWER, JOLENE McCOY, *Index*

*Overleaf: A Tasaday family of the Philippines waits in its cave
home for wild yams to roast. Page 1: Turkana herdsmen of Kenya
talk of cattle—from left, Lopirakori, Itiyen, Ezin. Endpapers:
Yąnomamö warriors of Venezuela dance before a feast. Bookbinding:
A Yąnomamö archer draws his powerful palmwood bow.*
OVERLEAF: JOHN LAUNOIS, BLACK STAR. PAGE 1: NEVILLE DYSON-HUDSON.
ENDPAPERS PHOTOMONTAGE AND BOOKBINDING SILHOUETTE FROM PHOTOGRAPHS
BY NAPOLEON A. CHAGNON.

JOHN SCOFIELD, NATIONAL GEOGRAPHIC STAFF

*Moss headdress, trimmed with cuscus fur
and beetles, frames the painted face
of a tribesman in the Mount Hagen
district of New Guinea. Symbols of
prestige, shell ornaments pierce his nose.*

FOREWORD

ALEXANDER POPE was not thinking of primitive peoples when he wrote: "The proper study of Mankind is Man." But he was too wise to ignore them; his *Essay on Man* includes some famous—if ill-informed—lines on the beliefs of the "poor Indian."

Today we recognize more and more clearly that the proper study of mankind cannot confine itself to civilizations. During the past century ethnologists have studied hundreds of nonliterate cultures, each with complex ways of patterned behavior derived from their ancestors. These scientific reports help us see what is distinctive about the way we organize the so-called advanced societies of our own day.

This book offers something that such technical reports seldom include: informal but authoritative accounts of how one goes about trying to understand a primitive society; what people say about their own customs; the welcome they offer—or the obstacles they set up; what it's like, in short, to live under social conditions so different from ours that the experience reminds the anthropologist of living in another era.

Neville Dyson-Hudson comments: " 'Lost in time' sounds like the glossy sort of romance—but it's literally true: just half a day's walk from a little administrative center, and it's a different age. Primitive people aren't literally lost, or lost in benightedness; if they're lost in anything, from our point of view, it's time. Or time is what we're both lost in, with respect to each other."

As we study the unique—often, to us, the bizarre—actions of members of these cultures, we should remember that everyone now alive on this globe belongs biologically to the same genus, *Homo,* and the same species, *sapiens.* Therefore it should not surprise us that what individuals everywhere do is related to certain universal human needs and interests.

All people, civilized or nonliterate, have special cultural ways of viewing birth and child rearing; special manners for the ingestion of food; special concerns for kinship and special ways of dealing with outsiders; special attitudes toward death. All show interest in the meaningful features of their world: living plants and animals; mountains and rivers; sun, moon, and stars. These factors lead beyond the realistic and adaptive responses necessary for the preservation of life, to the invention of explanations for observed phenomena, especially by the creation and transmission of myth.

This book gives impressive instances of the importance of myth in the lives of nonliterate peoples. We may think that science has replaced myth in our lives, but the work of contemporary scholars makes us wonder if we are as myth-free as we suppose. For example, Claude Lévi-Strauss, the distinguished anthropologist of the Collège de France, suggests that the myths of primitive peoples may give us a deep and new way of understanding some of the most puzzling aspects of our own inner life.

Thus one may read this book in a number of ways. Some will look at its carefully selected pictures and its informative paragraphs for the sheer pleasure of learning about the strange lifestyles of some of our most unfamiliar fellow human beings. Others will look at its chapters for clues to the workings of our own society, resemblances to and interpretations of our own behavior—in other words, for ways of following Pope's excellent dictum about the proper study of mankind.

Every reader, I believe, will find that the way we manage our own lives takes on new meaning as we consider other peoples of this planet—who because of geographical isolation or the caprice of history still lead lives that are at once amazingly similar and yet also amazingly different from our own.

LEONARD CARMICHAEL
Chairman, Committee for
Research and Exploration

CONTENTS

For Brazil's Cinta Larga Indians — as for innumerable other primitive people — high occasions demand high regalia: designs of paint; feathers; jewelry in profusion.

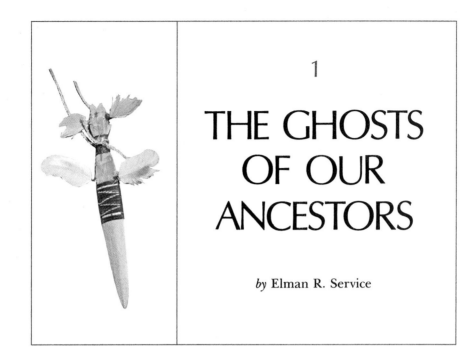

1

THE GHOSTS OF OUR ANCESTORS

by Elman R. Service

"Tʜᴀᴛ's — ᴛʜᴇ — ᴡᴀʏ — we — do." Hearing this again was too much. I rose painfully from the squat that I assumed in imitation of my Havasupai friend when he was giving me instruction. I stomped around on my prickling legs and said in near exasperation, "But why? Why?"

Paya looked up at me, silent, and I saw that I was discourteous to the old man by towering over him. I squatted and waited. Everything always took so long! He watched my face as though to be sure of my full attention. I looked into his eyes — watching, waiting.

The silence lingered, except for the sound of the falls and rapids as Havasu Creek rushed through its red-walled gorge toward the Grand Canyon. As usual, we had walked along the stream to be alone for our daily interview, away from his family and neighbors.

Clay-smeared and naked in mourning for his wife, a New Guinea tribesman on the Upper May River paddles a dugout homeward with his son.

Finally, never blinking, his seamed face calm, Paya repeated, "That's — the — way — we — do." He spoke even more slowly than usual. His normal English was halting, with dreamy spaces often conveying as much significance as his words. This illiterate old man prized exactly expressed thought, and he did not care how long it took to achieve it: the attitude of a respected wise-man. But this phrase, spoken so softly, held me in the same way that his unwavering gaze had stilled my movements.

My introduction to Havasupai culture was also an introduction to the mind of this man, and at first I was never sure which was which. Later I realized that his careful intensity of manner stemmed from concern that I, a messenger to the outside, should understand the ways of the Havasupai — not just his own. "The way *we* do."

I discovered still later that he was trying to teach me a simple idea of great significance, which I have tried to teach others for the past twenty-five years.

In our sessions he would describe in annoying detail how to do a curing ceremony, or plant corn, recite an origin myth, or calculate kinship. I dutifully took down

Chosen from the few primitive societies
that remain, these reveal cultural
patterns that assured human survival
for many thousands of years. They rank
as "primitive" by virtue of simple
technology, absence of formal government, life passed almost exclusively in
the company of kindred and always in
the presence of the supernatural.

the information, but impatiently. This was
my first fieldwork; I wanted some short
cuts, generalizations; above all, I wanted
to know the reasons *why* the Indians acted
in their peculiar ways. Paya answered:
"That's—the—way. . . ." Then he would go
back to the description as if I had mis-
understood the whole thing.

I was looking for a key to Havasupai culture, afraid of not finding it, and right
there I impatiently overlooked the truth:
*There is no key to understanding another cul-
ture except on its own terms.*

Paya was truly a man of two cultures and
this, I think now, was the basis of his wisdom. He had left his remote Arizona canyon as a youth to work as a cowboy. He
practiced his distinctive English and he
learned a surprising amount of what he
called American Ways. He had acquired by
himself an anthropological axiom: that a
custom can be understood only in its own
cultural setting.

Our sessions went so slowly because he

MRU

TASADAY

TIFALMIN

FORE

MBOTGATE

was patiently waiting for me to get a better grasp of this. He was saying that the 'Supai Ways, in themselves, were no easier to understand than the American Ways. He meant by "ways," of course, the patterns of behavior, of etiquette and ritual, the religious beliefs, the morality that people must accept to function as a society.

The ways of this isolated village — 250 people — were those of a primitive society. Aside from the influence of the lone U. S. Government agent, this was a society without government, police, judges, or jails; without industry or market; without formally organized religion or priesthood. These people were so self-sufficient because they were so interdependent. They took care of each other the way kinfolk should.

Paya would not have called these Ways inferior or superior to the American Ways, though he had chosen to end his days in the comfort of the culture of his own people. But that was psychic comfort. Life was harsh in the canyon and the people were ill-clad, often hungry, always malnourished. Their rich plots of farmland were too small for their numbers. Paya would readily acknowledge the material advantages of the American Ways. I thought he might welcome some of the physical comforts I could provide. I felt secure about this; who could ever fault sincere generosity?

Forewarned of the dire 'Supai poverty, my wife and I had brought a lot of worn clothing and blankets and utensils, to use and leave behind. We also had a large box of canned goods, which the people loved. Although the main products of the canyon were corn and peaches, the favorite delicacies from outside were canned cream of corn and canned peaches. We would signify our gratitude and friendship by leaving these things for the whole village.

BUT WHEN it came time to do it, we didn't know how. Finally, since Paya was a respected elder and our closest friend, we decided to leave everything with him. He would give it all away, 'Supai fashion, but gain much enjoyment and prestige by his giving. He was saddling the horses for our departure as my wife and I brought, in two trips, the bags of clothes, the utensils, and the heavy box of canned goods.

"My friend," I said, "don't pack these, they are for you." He nodded once, but didn't even look at me or the goods. Perhaps he hadn't understood.

I opened the sacks, pointed out the other things: "We're leaving these for you to dispose of as you like. I know I paid your wages; but now we want to give you these in addition, to our old friend."

I had talked too much, too fast. He carried the things into his mud-and-brush hut, but still no word. My wife and I felt badly rebuffed. We retreated to our camp and busied ourselves with packing. Now that he had been paid, was he showing openly his true dislike for us?

During the slow 14 miles up to the canyon rim, Paya was as affable as ever, in his dignified way. Yet he never referred to our gift, even during the affecting goodbye ritual with its steady searching gaze into the other's eyes — as though (I think) to memorize the person "inside." We tried not to show it, but our hurt was still a burden and now also a puzzle.

A few years later, when I was teaching anthropology at Columbia University, a leathery man of 50-some years came to my office and introduced himself as a missionary and engineer from a southwestern Indian reservation. He had come to New York to study and try to recover "enjoyment in helping fellow men." Did I give any courses that showed "how the Indian mind works"?

I said I thought not—"but let's talk about it. What's the trouble?"

"Well," he said, "I have given my whole career to this tribe. We've built dams and ditches and catch basins all over the place. Without my help they couldn't have made even one that would hold up. I always thought that I would understand them someday, and love them as God's children. But I don't understand them any better now than in the beginning! Less! And as for loving them, I'm ashamed to say it, but I cannot."

We discussed this; finally I asked, "Are you paid for your work?" "No," he said, "I have only my missionary living allowance. Nothing from the tribe. I have given my *life* to those people"—his voice, which had been rising, broke—"*and I have never received a word of thanks! Not ever!*"

I may have shouted or done a Plains Indian war dance. I remember stuttering and waving my arms. With difficulty, I calmed down: "I've got to tell you how my 'Supai friend wounded my wife and me." He listened carefully. To my joy he saw the point immediately: "I guess Indians just don't say 'Thanks.' I never thought of that. 'Thanks' seems like such a perfectly natural human response, but maybe it's only ours."

I spoke with the missionary several times after that, reporting new examples of the complications of expressing gratitude. Stories like the following just delighted him—he felt they were curing his malaise.

A Greenland Eskimo hunter was distributing portions of walrus meat, and he included the anthropologist Peter Freuchen, who thanked him lavishly. An old man corrected Freuchen: "You must not thank for your meat; it is your right to get parts. In this country, nobody wants to be dependent upon others. Therefore, there

Stone blade, split stick, and vine comprise a classic ax: tool and weapon of primitive peoples. A Cinta Larga Indian of Brazil made this specimen to hint for one of steel as a gift.

is nobody who gives or gets gifts, for thereby you become dependent. With gifts you make slaves just as with whips you make dogs!"

Later, the missionary wrote gratefully from the reservation that anthropology had indeed helped him, and I wrote back to remind him that it was really Paya.

I never achieved the full bicultural sophistication of Paya, but his example caused me to aim for it—and I am forever grateful. I think he insisted on "that's—the—way" partly because he felt he understood his own 'Supai customs better after his experience with American Ways. He implied that by learning his people's ways I could understand mine more fully. This was Paya's wisdom as I comprehend it now, much later. The best kind, surely: taking its time to sink in, but acquiring more significances, colors, and aspects as experience finds ever more uses for it.

AND I emphasize these stories of etiquette because in primitive life a person brings so much sensitivity to all personal relations. I had never lived in such a closed-in community, and in my ignorance I had associated etiquette with Emily Post's "polite society"—hence my mistakes.

Like a great many people in my generation in the U.S.A., I had grown up in a small town. Like the wistful boy of Sherwood Anderson's fictional Winesburg, Ohio, I yearned to escape from the prison of hometown watchful gossip to the freedom of urban life. This is a familiar story.

But now imagine yourself in a much smaller community, of relatives only—from whom you have no escape whatever! You belong to this group for life, and you know it. You must achieve all your aspirations—to be respected as great or good or wise—on this one stage, before this tiny unchanging audience. Your social mistakes might be costly, since you can never simply "leave town," and you avoid them by carefully following the accepted patterns of behavior.

In primitive society everything is personal. There are no such abstractions as crime, for example, or such institutions as courts. A "bad thing" is something one person has done to another. The victim may seek his own redress. If the bad deed has wronged a member of another kin group, the two groups involve themselves in the problem. No third party of justice speaks impersonal dooms to the guilty.

But even with the dominance of an outside power, problems arise. I remember when a woman shot and killed her husband, in a primitive village I won't name. The state demanded her imprisonment "in the name of the law." But the villagers refused to give her up: she wasn't guilty! She had been drunk. As her true self she wouldn't have killed her husband, and would never kill anyone again. She would never drink again! She had suffered enough; it was, after all, her own husband she had lost, and she loved him.

This community might have punished a lack of generous public spirit, in a normal person, more severely. Yet precisely because the common good is all-important, a social failure may be lived down, proved to be a mistake, or wiped out in rituals that restore good feeling and good humor.

A high good humor often marks the sociability of primitive societies. We notice the absence of TV and radio and cinema, and conclude that primitive people must entertain themselves. But I think the source of enjoyment lies deeper than the fun of the activity; it lies in the shared appreciation of companions.

What has struck me in primitive societies, above all, is the total irrelevance of my wristwatch to the life around me. We think of a time to work and a time to play, and the lack of time for as much play or rest as we want. In all primitive communities I have visited, work-time merges into playtime—or, better, no one really distinguishes the two.

Most ordinary tasks are done in sociable enjoyment, and the more people involved, the more it reminds me of an old-time rural barn raising or quilting bee.

Sometimes an all-hands emergency arises —haying before a rain, a sudden run of fish to be netted all night long, migrating caribou to be intercepted—demanding incredible bursts of energy, with terrible physical punishments, all endured uncomplainingly. Some of the best of good times occur in the aftermath.

I remember a cattle roundup by Paraguayan Indians, dangerous and exhausting work in temperatures that split my head although I was only watching. But after the work was done they spent the next day playing at it, with games of horsemanship.

I was invited to ride in a sprint race along level bottomland by a river, and given a horse that turned out to be unbroken. It tried to run right out from under me; we won the race and then some. I strained at the hackamore but the horse dashed on, scattering people and cattle until at a sudden meander it slowed down belly-deep in the water and I gratefully dumped myself off. Laughter—and some commiseration—welcomed me back, and the games went on.

Whatever the occasion, all this primitive sufficiency of time seems to flow in companionship. People are seldom alone; to work alone with Paya I had to walk a couple of miles along Havasu Creek. Every ethnologist I've ever asked had the same reaction to the first full experience with life in a primitive community: "How come they don't get on each other's nerves? It's *all* so intimate!" How "un-American" it was, how unfree!

Since pioneer times on the frontier, Americans have extolled personal freedom and individualism. Above all, we associate these ideals with privacy. We want to own private cars, to own a suburban house as distant from others as possible, to give the children "a room of one's own."

But it is from the families who can afford such privacy that the complaints of alienation and loneliness come. Cults of communal living and "encounter groups" arise in response, a quest for trust and intimacy. Whatever their success, do they offer a way to the satisfactions of primitive life? I'm sure Paya would say no, and I have learned enough to agree with him.

Volunteers, free to stay or go at will, may cooperate to create a good society, but certainly not a primitive one.

All primitive communities—bands, clans, camps, villages—are essentially families in a general sense. And surely the most repressive institution in any society must be the family. But with this family tyranny we find the truest, most purely altruistic, and most constant form of love: that of parents for their children.

With each kin relationship we find authority and love in various mixtures. In primitive societies these variations regulate all of the social life there is. Each person benefits from love until death, and remains a lifelong prisoner of authority. Thus social

In Bangladesh hill country, a girl of the Mru tribe checks cleaned rice for chaff or grit before cooking—a daily chore.

CLAUS-DIETER BRAUNS

life becomes complex indeed; I have found it almost unbearably so.

We may lament the complexity of America, but it gives us escape routes from home and parents or other emotional entanglements. We can change neighborhoods, even cities, and jobs, clubs, friends. One can even choose whom to marry, or never marry—unimaginable freedoms in most of the world's societies today and in most of its history.

In primitive societies we notice repressions and inequalities, but these spring from the family itself, from roles of age and sex, ancient, traditional, and therefore consistent. Thus members of the family do not see them as matters of choice, and probably do not feel as unfree as we think.

Let me try to be as objective as Paya. Some good things and some bad things go with primitive communities. Many young people today want to study primitive society because they feel dissatisfied with our own. They long for the secure love, trust, and cooperation that Rousseau attributed to his "noble savages." Who does not?

But do we want the other side of the coin: the unending submission to parental authority, the lifelong togetherness of the extended family; not even a brief vacation with its chance for a few social adventures?

I disagree with some of our American Ways, even loathe some of them; but I cannot imagine adjusting permanently to the life of a primitive group. I would much prefer to live insecurely in the culture of Winesburg, Ohio, with the dream of making it to Toledo someday.

If primitive society provides so few individual choices, and if our society provides too many, could we achieve some compromise by mixing the two? Sad to say, this clearly is not possible.

This book describes essentials of primitive culture. No society has preserved these and at the same time adapted itself to modern civilization. Nor has primitive culture as yet significantly modified that civilization, beyond its strong influence on the art of this century.

One of the most isolated, most pristinely aboriginal of human societies, is that of the Tasaday, recently discovered in the Philippine Islands. Generations ago, frightened by contacts with outsiders, their ancestors must have retreated and hidden to save themselves and their ways.

Now they have been photographed, interviewed, measured—and inevitably their gentle society is doomed. It is too late; they have been met and they are ours.

As an organization based on kinship, primitive society is politically fragile even when isolated. A North American Indian once summed up the limits of authority in his tribe: "One word from the chief—and everybody does just as he pleases!" Commenting on his experience with the fierce Yąnomamö of Venezuela, my old friend and collaborator Napoleon Chagnon says, "A large village is like a powderkeg—and the wrong word from anybody can set it off."

A society adjusted to outsiders remains vulnerable to economic forces. The Batammaba (or "Somba") of Dahomey represent a culture resting on complicated relationships to other kinds of African societies and later to a colonial administration. Sometimes an outside force does something virtuous; here the French brought peace to a troubled countryside.

But the French also brought cash crops and currency, taxes to pay and new things to buy. The primitive ideology survives among the Somba—in all-pervasive supernaturalism and complicated rituals—but desire for products of the industrial-commercial world can disrupt such a community drastically.

Stresses about wealth may pervade a primitive group remote from a cash economy. "It's hard to stay rich," laments Neville Dyson-Hudson's Turkana friend Loceyto —whose family begins with 5 wives and 25 children and includes 2 brothers with wives and offspring: all with claims on him. Generosity is never simple.

B E GENEROUS . . . but perhaps there is no such thing as a "pure" gift. "Gifts make slaves." In primitive societies giving away a surplus or sharing resources is prudence, like a bank deposit. Someday you will need something the recipient can give you; you will receive it. Everyone depends on these customary rights of reciprocity.

Confidence in such rights seems high, at seasons of great abundance or abject scarcity. In Tarahumara groups of northwest Mexico, among people close to starvation, I never noticed any competition or selfishness that I could attribute to the scarcity. Missionaries (with our small contributions) gave what they could—corn or beans. We never saw anyone hoard this or hide it.

Thus a sort of lifeboat economics prevails, a spirit of we're-all-in-this-together.

This have-not, want-not complacency, with its sharing of available goods, shatters in the proximity of civilization. With another Mexican tribe, I have seen hoarding — and felt that not only the hungry individuals but also the culture itself had come near death.

Undoubtedly Paya knew that the peace of his beautiful canyon was in danger from alien products. This may be a reason why he didn't look at our gifts to him. Perhaps he couldn't look, because of what they symbolized. How long would it be before his people would keep money and goods for themselves, as measures of prestige?

So many primitive peoples, if not most, unwittingly hasten the demise of their own society in favor of material gains. With the end of their isolation comes insecurity, and can anyone who truly imagines that insecurity blame them for what they do?

Yet I must confess that I find the simplicity of their material life very appealing, with its good-fellowship and its lack of envy and cupidity. To be sure, I want all people in the world fed and doctored properly; but I always come back to my sharp memory of a splendid group of Macá Indians in the Gran Chaco of Paraguay, sporting breechclouts and brilliant headdresses of feathers — and a few empty wristwatches, worn, I hope, with contempt for such things except as funny ornaments.

All primitive cultures that we know about — and those included in this book are representative — are alike in certain respects that obviously contrast with much of our urban, industrialized society. Ours is very new to the human race, and evidently stiff and uncomfortable. Of all human existence, 99 percent was life in primitive society, as a fraction remains today. If for no other reason than this, we should be curious about it.

Wholehearted and distinctive in primitive societies is the supernaturalism that completely envelops all existence. In this book, the chapters on the Mbotgate and the Tifalmin illustrate this beautifully.

This is not religion in the sense of faith in the truth of the teachings of a master. Primitive belief in the powers of the unseen, of ancestral spirits and creator-gods, is not a matter of faith. You are not converted to it. You accept it because it is an integral part of the culture into which you were born, as pervasive and unquestioned as the grammar of your language.

When a missionary converts members of a primitive society, it alters that distinctive unity of culture — inevitably, and irreversibly. It may foretell the culture's collapse or disintegration. Not even in spiritual matters is generosity simple.

If only we could find reciprocity with primitive societies! We offer both goods and faith to them, but we have not accepted their gift of clues to our own past — to distinguish what is "perfectly natural human response" from what is "only ours."

When a primitive culture is lost, all mankind loses, for the human race has not begun to learn from it. We have not yet understood enough about mankind at large, about the numerous forms his culture can take, or the reasons for them, or the elemental basis of his universality.

I believe this to be true, as another anthropologist once said: "Ever since their discovery by an expanding European civilization, primitive peoples have continued to hover over thoughtful men like ancestral ghosts. . . ."

Today especially we need to consider their presence. Perhaps it offers the best gift we can receive, from the primitive peoples who are our contemporary ancestors.

What, after all, is the most precious gift your ancestors, your parents and their parents before them, would want to give you? Love, obviously. But with the gift of ancestral love comes ancestral authority. And its purpose is the noblest and most important of all: to instruct you in the arts of survival — whether you like it or not.

In this case, the gift takes form as the wisdom that comes from understanding your own ways better by knowing theirs.

For this uncomfortable but most important knowledge I am indebted to Paya and to the Havasupai culture that he made a living part of my life. I wish I could have given him in return something more inspiring than canned corn and worn pants.

His face bound by bark strips, a Fore man of New Guinea blackens his lips for a boy's initiation. The matchbox in his leaf-and-fur regalia suggests the ease — and extent — of modern influence as recently as 1963.

In the rugged New Guinea Highlands, the Fore slash and burn tracts of virgin forest to establish small hamlet-garden complexes— adapting to their environment, as primitive societies must. Today, adapting to change, they grow coffee for cash as well as subsistence crops; square family houses reflect the impact of Australian administration. Sitting under a bark cape, a mother wears strands of trade beads from missionaries along with seed necklaces.

E. RICHARD SORENSON

Famous since their first encounter with the outside world, in 1971, Tasaday children peer from rock niches by their cave home, deep in the mountainous rain forest of Mindanao in the Philippines. The Tasaday, only 24 in number when discovered, gather food in abundance with the simple but sufficient skills and tools of the Stone Age. They live without worry, fear little except disease, want nothing except wives for the bachelors. Fire provides the luxury of warmth for a youngster named Lubu, content, like his people, in a land of plenty.

Silhouetted among vines and bamboo, frolicsome Lubu blends with a setting little altered by his band. His father, Bilangan, scrapes a roasted wild yam while his mother nurses his brother Ilib. Perched on father's shoulders, three-year-old Seol studies a wild blossom — a food item for the Tasaday. The government of the Philippines has set aside 50,000 acres to save their forest home from logging.

JOHN LAUNOIS, BLACK STAR

Bow drawn, arrow nocked and aimed, a Cinta Larga Indian of Brazil's rich
wilderness sights a fish stupefied by sap from lengths of vine called timbo.
Another twirls a stick to start a fire in dry tinder; smoking out wild bees
yields a trove of honey. Hunter-gatherers, estimated at 3,000 to 5,000 in
number and named in Portuguese for the belts worn by the men, the Cinta Larga
apparently grow manioc, peanuts, and corn. Threatened by land developers
and by disease, they defy a pacification mission to protect them. They have
accepted—and sometimes arrogantly seized—tools and trinkets offered in
friendship. In return they have given ornaments, seeds, and arrows, a sign of
trust, but these proud warriors have barred outsiders from their villages.

JESCO VON PUTTKAMER

Passing beneath the baobab tree, Dogon women of the West African nation of Mali bear water from the plain to their village. Gourd dippers bob in the tub, a market purchase, and the deftly balanced clay canari *that holds approximately five gallons and weighs some 40 pounds full. Subsistence farmers, the 250,000 Dogon live along the Cliffs of Bandiagara, a 600-foot-high sandstone escarpment; their mud dwellings and granaries nestle in its cave-pocked face. Fleeing hostile tribes more than 600 years ago, the Dogon took over these easily defended heights —and villages built by dwarfs with sticky hands according to tribal legend.*

PAMELA JOHNSON MEYER

Skirts rustling, Dogon men dancing in cowrie-shell masks embody animal or human spirits in a dama, *a dramatic ceremony commending the soul of a deceased village elder to the world of his ancestors. The Dogon hold fast to numerous and elaborate rites such as this one, which ends a year or more of formal mourning.*

Overleaf: A Mru tribesman threshes with his feet the rice that women reap on a hillside cleared by slash and burn. Whatever their diligence, valley harvests surpass theirs. Mru justify their poverty and illiteracy by myth—a cow sent as messenger ate the banana-leaf Scriptures giving their great spirit Torai's rules for life.

CLAUS-DIETER BRAUNS

2

MBOTGATE

Heirs to a verdant land,
survivors of troubled years

by E. Richard Sorenson
Photographs by Sam Abell
and the author

HE WAS ALWAYS alert to the actions and expressions of the people around him; and, catching my glance from the sunlit coast of Malekula Island to that gray darkness over its mountainous interior, my interpreter Metak repeated that Mbotgate phrase, now all too familiar: "*Ausa usa —* it's raining."

He knew I found that saturated atmosphere hard to take. The air dampened everything: clothes, sleeping bags, cameras.

Switching to Bislama, the pidgin of the New Hebrides, Metak continued: "Malekula emi ples igat planti ren. Be klosap solwora igat san. Bek long ples insaid emi blak olgeta taem. — It rains a lot here in Malekula, but near the ocean there's sun. Back in the mountains it's black all the time."

Hidden under those clouds was a sanctuary of traditional inland life in the New Hebrides, the homeland of the people who speak the Mbotgate language or the Nab-

Wearing leaves often used in dances,
a tribesman carries bow, arrows, and a
club — relic of war. Mbotgate live by
hunting, gathering, and gardening.

wal. (European residents on the coast call these people and others "Small Nambas," referring to the style of leaf penis sheath worn by the men.) Few outsiders had penetrated the area of the Mbotgate, and their culture center remained isolated until 1968, when my friend Kal Muller, attracted by rumors of a population still living by its own primitive ways, struggled up into these mountains from South-West Bay.

Impressed by the way of life he saw, and aware of its importance to studies of human behavior and human potential, Kal suggested I come for anthropological reconnaissance. In 1971 he showed me the route in, from the coastal village of Butin, where people profess Christianity now.

The next year I returned with Joan Mossman, a Ph.D. candidate in anthropology from Stanford University, to help her get established for her fieldwork here. Throughout Melanesia, the South Pacific islands from Fiji west through New Guinea, highly varied societies had developed before Europeans came; we would have one of the last opportunities to observe a culture that has not adopted Western ways.

We could expect certain things that are

Steep, densely forested ranges in the heartland of Malekula provide a citadel of pagan tradition in the New Hebrides: cloud-veiled villages of the Mbotgate. Like culturally related groups, this one bears the Europeans' name "Small Nambas," a reference to the garb of men.

widespread in Melanesia: subsistence crops and highly valued pigs; a culture without inherited rank, where men must earn status; belief in sorcery; secret societies of men. We could learn some facts fairly quickly, but only with time and long study can we hope for genuine understanding.

There are six ceremonial centers in these mountains, four of Mbotgate-speakers and two of Nabwal, with scattered hamlets. The total population may be less than 150, its density 2 per square mile at most.

It was not always like this. Older Mbotgate remember a quite different time, when more people lived here and more languages were spoken. But they claim that in a "time of troubles" death and destruction stalked the land.

Contagious diseases have struck the New Hebrides repeatedly in the past century, and oral history indicates that within living memory an epidemic took heavy toll of the Mbotgate—which implies a lack of immunity caused by isolation. The effect was evidently disastrous.

Where ideas of sorcery explain illness and ill fortune as the result of human malice, men readily see their sufferings as overwhelming proof of a vicious covert campaign against them—by their neighbors. They react to protect themselves.

Miliun, oldest and most influential man of Yabgatass village, tells of great sickness, bitter fighting, desperate attacks to discourage sorcery or scatter the suspects. Some villages were wiped out, others abandoned when their residents fled.

During this period the Mbotgate became masters of the region. They survived the epidemics; they did not leave. Miliun says they were the best fighters. Their Nabwal allies also remained. But they recognized the Mbotgate as pre-eminent, and the village of Lendombwey as the spiritual and ceremonial center of the area. Today the mountains are peaceful, the epidemics past.

I am not certain whether my friend Metak and his fellow villagers in Butin were refugees from this "time of troubles" or came later in quest of a new way of life. They settled there only a decade ago, when Metak was about 12—old enough to have learned the mountain ways but not to have made enemies. Unlike his fellows he occasionally went back, unafraid.

He could carry bigger loads than anyone else, go farther and faster over more difficult trails. No hardship seemed to dent his sense of humor. He was truly a man of the mountains. But he also knew the coastal ways and was acquainted with Western man. He bridged these cultures; he connected two epochs. It was a stroke of incredible luck to have found him.

How do you gain acceptance or welcome in a primitive society? With Metak to vouch for me I could move forthrightly into the Mbotgate villages, where everyone knew him. I did not have to roam cautiously from place to place, searching for somewhere to begin work, or play the role of a one-man sideshow with exciting things from an outside world of material riches.

ULTIMATELY, acceptance or welcome depends on how much interest your presence attracts. People may show you tolerance because they value hospitality. They may let you stay because of what you bring, how they think you might help them, or how much they simply enjoy novelties.

In some places I have been welcome just as a new face among people who rarely see anyone they haven't known all their lives. But the promise of new goods and knowledge is usually a stronger card. In the New Guinea Highlands, during the 1950's and '60's, groups would compete for the presence of Europeans as emissaries from their ancestors, bringing unprecedented material reward. In other parts of New Guinea I have been welcomed as a protection against attack and sorcery; elsewhere, simply because I made friends with the children.

Just what the Mbotgate would make of our presence, I didn't know, but I had learned that facial expressions of emotion vary only in part from culture to culture. I would watch closely for signs of fear, disgust, anger—or happiness.

With Metak and an apprehensive crew of porters from Butin, Joan and I started inland. Darkness overtook us on the last steep ascent to tiny Yabgatass, where the trail grew wider, muddier, and more slippery. Of course no one in the village was expecting our arrival, and they had shut themselves into their warm, smoky, windowless houses for the night by piling logs and sticks across the entrance.

But the barricades soon came down, and people came out to gape. Miliun appeared suddenly in the mist, coming down from the *nakamal*, residence and ceremonial house of men, taboo to outsiders.

In 1971 Miliun seemed basically helpful, but uncommunicative and shy. Anthropologists on a return visit often find people more cordial—this time Miliun beamed as he saw us, and shortly offered some of the taro pudding called *laplap*, hot from the fire. This was a good omen, for among Melanesians food sharing is usually an expression of genuine good will.

He offered an abandoned but livable house to shelter our porters, and space in his own house for Metak and me. But I had taken shelter there once before, and picked up a number of lice and fleas. Joan and I preferred tents—an astonishing novelty, since even our porters had not seen a portable house before.

Placing of houses follows no definite pattern here. Our tent site was the flat yard between Miliun's house and the nearby "woman's house" of one of his wives. Mbotgate men and women do not share the same house; as in much of Melanesia, men shun such close contact with women in order to avoid "contamination" and to preserve strength, health, and manliness. Next day Miliun selected a site between his house and the nakamal, and Metak persuaded nine of our porters to build a house there for Joan.

On our third night in Yabgatass, I was about to get into my sleeping bag when I heard Miliun intermittently humming and muttering to himself. I took some tobacco out to give him and sat with him in his doorway, facing the side of my tent. He seemed fascinated by it. Light from a kerosene lamp inside created a diffuse overall glow through the thin orange nylon. A white panel at the bottom made a luminous foundation that gave a strange, weightless, almost ethereal appearance in the mist. It was spectacular even to me.

Shadows from things inside, and from reinforcement seams, showed as black; and I recognized in them a luminous accidental face that curiously resembled the cult art of the Mbotgate. I was impressed; Miliun was spellbound. We sat, silently staring at it. Finally I went back inside and went to sleep. How long Miliun remained there, what he was thinking, I don't know.

Next day he began working on the house, strengthening the joints with vines and bringing leaves for thatch from the jungle. Other Mbotgate men began to pitch in. This was welcome help, since the coastal men were complaining of the weather and of sorcery. One had an inflamed eye; he

confided that a woman had caused it by throwing leaves toward him. I paid them, and they hastened away. Sections of roof went up just in time—my tent succumbed to the rains, and Joan and I had to work frantically to salvage the wet gear. I had to take shelter in the house, and assume that the villagers would consider this just one more aspect of our strangeness.

Joan has special opportunities here, although this may seem strange in a village where formal and ceremonial life is based on the men's secret society, the *nimangi*. Youths enter it by formal initiations, and rise by grade-taking ceremonies to higher knowledge of its secret lore. As an alien I cannot learn much about it.

Mbotgate women, and the Nabwal women who sometimes come as wives, may not see its art and must act as if they know nothing about it. But they live in a very small community. Drawing on my New Guinea experience, I assume that in fact they know a good deal. Since men marry women from other villages, Joan and I reasoned that women might share their knowledge with someone like themselves: another woman, another outsider.

Moreover, Mbotgate women have developed a nimangi society of their own, with initiations and grade-taking ceremonies parallel to the men's. This is something I hadn't seen in other Melanesian cultures, a sort of Melanesian women's lib, possibly an imitation of the men's society or a defense against it. Only a woman can carry out any detailed inquiry on this.

Whenever I came around, the women were always a little nervous, but they soon became quite friendly with Joan. They seemed particularly pleased by her eager efforts to learn their language and spontaneously gave her words for things. I am a little jealous—the men are more reticent.

Their skills spoke for themselves, however, when I visited Lendombwey, the culture center—about four hours' fast walk on a trail with only one long climb. Metak, a stalwart young man named Kamanleever, carrying his bow and arrows, and a man from Lendombwey went with me. We had

As only men and boys may do, four-year-old Sari plays a resonant slit gong, nam'bulukai, *a signaling device as well as an integral part of ritual life.*

not been on the trail long when the whine of wings caught my ear. It barely registered in my brain. But Metak was transformed, taut and still like a man possessed, ready to stalk a quarry. So Metak is a hunter, I thought. But he had no weapon and his mood passed quickly.

When we sat down to rest at a place where the jungle was thinner, Kamanleever came up with a large dove-like bird suspended from a stick over his shoulder. Metak, looking pleased but not surprised, disappeared for a few minutes and returned with bananas and coconuts. The man from Lendombwey pulled a leaf-wrapped packet out of his waistband and produced several freshwater shrimp. A feast was taking shape, and I was impressed by how quickly and sumptuously wild foods were provided for us. I had assumed that the Mbotgate were not just subsistence gardeners; obviously they were also quite competent hunter-gatherers.

Metak asked me for matches. The damp had got to them; they didn't work. But two pieces of wood from the jungle made a fire; soon we had a good blaze.

The dove was plucked and gutted, wrapped in leaves, and put into the fire. I noted the recipe for a kind of natural casserole—slit the peel of a banana, keeping the skin as intact as possible; mash the pulp with coconut milk; add a shrimp; using vine, tie the peel around the contents; set the package in the fire; cook until done.

A relaxed efficiency marked all these preparations, and the bird was unusually delicious, neither tough nor gamey.

At LENDOMBWEY, as at Yabgatass, residential offshoots scatter outward into the countryside from the ceremonial center. When old garden sites lose fertility, new ones must be cleared; and new houses are sometimes built near them. Only the ceremonial nakamals seem to have any aura of permanence, and possibly all the present settlements were founded by groups that left the vicinity of Lendombwey for new localities in the jungle.

Warm and moist, the jungle grows rapidly, moving against clearings and trails like an oil slick at sea tightening around patches of clear water. Adults and even children continually whack and slice at the vegetation with sticks or machetes as they walk along a trail. There doesn't seem to be any sense of duty involved—

just a kind of enjoyable preoccupation, a habit of life which has its value to life.

Even the thick jungle could not mute the call that alerted me one morning to an incident of special interest for my work: "Eeeyah, eeeyah." It was four-year-old Sari's trademark. Only he among the Yabgatass children made that noise, and he made it frequently—when he was surprised or frightened, when excited in play.

I study child behavior and development, and the specific patterns these take among children in different cultures, and this noise summoned me to watch a chasing game with Yelik and Galitneman, both older boys. (In such small villages close age-mates are not always available). They were trying to entice Sari into chasing them and jumping on them—and they never ran so fast or so far that he could not catch them from time to time.

With its deception and surprise attack, this looked like an aggressive kind of play. But it never erupted in squabbles or hostility. I saw no effort to excel others—as American children so often attempt to do. Good will did not get lost in the spirited action. A game of agility and cunning, it suits a culture where hunting contributes a sizable proportion of the food.

The next day I chanced upon Sari at the edge of the village clearing. Alone and quiet, deeply preoccupied, he ignored my approach. He was stalking lizards with Yelik's bow and arrow. Stealthily, in total silence, slowly, he skirted bushes and trees, each movement perfectly controlled. Spying a quarry, he drew his bowstring, muscles taut for a moment—and then the arrow flew. A miss. No sign of regret or disappointment. He simply retrieved his arrow and resumed his hunt.

His next shot nailed a lizard to the ground, impaled on one of the four prongs of the arrow. Not a trace of childlike exuberance at this success; no cries of "I got him!" Nor did he even look around to see who might have witnessed the great deed. Instead, with head slightly bowed and feet stamping, he rhythmically made a tight circle. It must have been some kind of Mbotgate victory dance that he had seen men perform. Then Sari retrieved the arrow with the lizard.

As in other primitive societies, children acquire virtually all their learning in their play. They play near adults at work, and with the implements adults use. On my first visit to the Mbotgate I saw a woman give her infant son a sharp knife to hold for her; startled, I had to suppress an impulse to intervene. Now I have concluded that such incidents are commonplace here.

Toddlers casually grab knives, machetes, burning sticks. They wave these around and carry them about without so much as a blink from nearby elders. Even babies snatch knives from their mothers. The Mbotgate view all this as normal; and only rarely do their children hurt themselves.

I have seen similar behavior among non-Westernized peoples elsewhere. But, here again, I wondered how small children could be so safe, yet so free. Why did "neglect" not endanger even toddlers? Questions like this had brought me here; but it will take time to learn the answers.

Some details of growing up among the Mbotgate became clear to me through Galitneman. About 12, he was the youngest male in Yabgatass to wear the nambas. He had been initiated, circumcised and purified from "contaminations" of living with his mother. Too young for a house of his own, he slept in the nakamal. One morning I found him outside my house in the rain, plaiting flattened bamboo into wall sections as he had seen the coastal natives do. It was a technique alien to the Mbotgate.

He looked embarrassed when he saw me watching; he gave his work a slight contemptuous kick and came to join me. But I had noted how competently he handled the bamboo, with an ability I could not equal. I "knew" the principle of plaiting, but he had a better feel for the reality. I could explain, he could do.

Deciding to investigate Galitneman's approach to novelty, I remembered that he had watched me change the film in my Nikon camera. Quickly I finished off a roll. Then, nodding at the Nikon and a new box of film, I glanced from them to Galitneman —a gesture to invite participation.

He took the camera, glancing tentatively at me. He seemed reassured as I ignored him. Just as I would have done, he removed the camera back, took out the exposed film, threaded the new film onto the take-up reel, replaced the back, and clicked off two frames. "An impressive perform-

Cult mask made of wood and clay, kept secret from women's eyes, goes on casual display for a man's camera.

ance," I thought—even if rote copying.

Galitneman had seen my attempts to light a new model of kerosene pressure stove. I had an instruction book, but once I failed to close the pressure valve and another time I had a mixture of flaming kerosene and alcohol erupt over my hands.

I decided to let him try his hand with this beast. I gave him the matches and nodded toward the stove. He seemed reluctant; but he lighted it without mishap. He had correctly judged which of my actions were essential; he did not copy my mistakes.

These incidents created a bond between us, and I was surprised when he refused a plate of tinned meat I offered him. But he turned his head aside and averted his eyes, a Melanesian gesture for rejection. Then, as if embarrassed, he quietly went away.

Returning the next morning, he looked around for a can of meat, picked it up, and said in perfectly clear Bislama—the first I heard from him—"Emi tabu blong mi."

Undoubtedly he had gone to Metak to learn this phrase, so he could explain that he was observing a meat prohibition. Just why and how long, I did not discover during my short visit; most likely the reasons are embedded in secret nimangi rules.

Once he started trying pidgin phrases, Galitneman kept coming back with more. About midmorning a few days later, he said to me, "Yu laik lukim samting?" He motioned for me to follow him, and we started up a trail on which I had seen only men and boys—never women or girls. Something intangible in the way he moved hinted at secrecy.

We hadn't gone far when he stopped abruptly at a tiny clearing cut since the day before. I didn't notice, at first, that Kamanleever was piling wood for a fire, working hastily but without the faintest clatter of sticks. A quiet that seemed a little eerie pervaded the atmosphere.

I watched for a few minutes, maybe longer. What seemed strange soon seemed boring. The sky was threatening rain; I turned to go. But Galitneman blocked the trail, so I turned again to watch Kamanleever just in time to see him throw a tied-up squirming piglet onto a growing fire as casually as if it were another stick of wood.

Reluctant to credit my senses, I looked at Galitneman. He was standing as if nothing had happened, without a hint of revulsion.

A distracting unreality settled over the scene. The pig made no noise. "At least it's unconscious," I thought. Then a frightened, bewildered whimpering began and turned by increments into a panic-stricken wail. Its crescendo broke in hoarse wheezes and spasmodic gasps, as if the animal was so disordered by the pain that it was drowning in its own terror.

I began to feel slightly dizzy: I saw Kamanleever calmly maneuver the piglet's head into the worst of the flames.

Suddenly the pig gave such a lurch that it scattered the fire. A second convulsion broke the rope around its hindlegs; and before Kamanleever could react, it had pushed its way out of the pile of sticks, tumbling headlong over its bound forelegs.

Then the rain came. Galitneman left. I followed, he to the nakamal, I to my house. When the rain abated and he came back, half an hour later, I had loaded my camera, hoping to get some kind of objective record of this.

Back at the clearing we found Kamanleever trying to get the fire going again. The pig was pressing its seared head and neck against some damp earth it had rooted up. Then into the fire again with the piglet, more convulsions and more squealing. It was too much for me and I left. Nothing in my culture had prepared me to be at ease in the face of this.

Later I learned from Metak that the affair was a plot by the men, to intimidate the women. According to him, men say that irate spirits may carry away and torture a pig belonging to a woman who has offended the ancestors.

Mbotgate women make special pets of baby pigs, lavishing affection on them. By the fiction that ancestors' spirits will attack the piglets, men seek to control the behavior of women by indirect threats. Probably a more direct threat would disrupt the social order, and this technique only requires men to be callous about pigs.

I sat in my house speculating: What was it in Mbotgate culture that could produce this kind of callousness? Certainly in other respects these people showed themselves tolerant, sympathetic, and generous. I even wondered if such contradictions are a mark of the primitive. And yet in our own Western culture we also tacitly condone brutality when alternatives are not clear to us, or when open recognition of it would challenge our self-respect. . . .

Obviously these "innocent primitives" are no more primitively innocent than we are. Simply dividing human beings into "primitive" and "civilized" is too simple. . . .

Metak cut short my reflections: "Emi gat wanpela emi klosap ded." Someone was critically ill, possibly close to death. He indicated that I should go with him. I did not hesitate; long ago I had learned to provide whatever relief I could to the isolated people I stayed with. I got my medicines. Off I went with Metak, Galitneman, Kamanleever, and a man named Kamanlik.

At the house of Intamas, one of Miliun's wives, I paused to adjust my eyes to the perpetual smoky darkness. A tension I had not felt before among the Mbotgate hung in the air, along with the smell of vomit. My flashlight revealed the rigid figure of Amogenendam propped halfseated against another woman. Rivulets of vomit trickled down her body into her grass skirt.

I reached for her pulse. Its strong regularity belied her apparent comatose state. I tried unsuccessfully to lift an eyelid; she was holding it closed. "Either she's hysterical or faking," I concluded.

Since something was expected of me, I took some water in a bamboo tube, smashed an aspirin in it, and gave it to Intamas to administer. Then Kamanlik came in with a firebrand in one hand, his cheeks puffed out and distended. Deliberately, almost officiously, he approached Amogenendam. An aerosol-like stream of green particles spewed from his mouth across the glowing brand onto her still-rigid body.

Rather in awe of this dramatic display, not knowing what to make of it or how to behave, I watched as Kamanlik emptied his cheeks of finely chewed leaf until Amogenendam was almost covered with green flecks. Then he left.

Walking back to my house, I asked Metak, "Emi laek mekem wanem samting? — What was he doing?"

"Emi meresin blong emi klosap ded — It's medicine for someone dying."

The next day I saw Amogenendam in Mwasak's house. She looked perfectly healthy as she wove a mat with some other women. Later that day I learned that the piglet burned to death had been hers.

Perhaps I was more persistent than usual when I asked Metak for details of these events. But on this subject he had become a blank wall. Obviously he did not want to discuss it with anyone in Yabgatass. He had better sense than to pry into matters so charged with emotion. I didn't press him.

I valued his friendship—and I wanted to maintain my welcome among the Mbotgate.

I can see reasons why they remain in their rainy highlands. Cool breezes make gardening a pleasant business. On the coast hot weather makes it hard work, and swarms of flies and malaria-carrying mosquitoes spread infection. Apparently the southern coast was thinly settled before Westernization brought mosquito nets and medicines. Even today the people there seem prone to illness, listless and dispirited in contrast to those of the mountains.

Still, there is more to the Mbotgate choice of interior villages than comfort and health. The Mbotgate nakamals proved their strength during the "time of troubles," and their members are now the uncontested beneficiaries of an abundant land. They do not yet think of themselves as inferior "bush people." Instead, they consider themselves superior to people like the coastals who have no nakamals. They take pride in their strong ancestor spirits, and make elegant and powerful artistic representations of them.

Yet, ironically, trade in these art objects fosters a growing contact with the coastal villages and people from the world beyond. From this contact I can foresee the end of a culture evolved over centuries: A strange and spirited people will shed their exotic way of life, which brought me here and of which we know so little.

The day after the healing of Amogenendam was my last in Yabgatass, but Joan is continuing her work among the Mbotgate. Already she has passed on to me information clarifying the episode that Galitneman had led me to see.

Less than a year ago, Amogenendam's husband died at Butin. She must remain chaste for a year, lest his spirit trouble the living—for her to step into the bush alone might be suspicious enough to incur a sanction as severe as torturing her pet.

So, from one incident to another, the logic of a society makes itself apparent and shapes the lives of individuals. I plan to return to the Mbotgate to study their ways of rearing children—and see what time will bring for toddlers like little Legas and boys like Yelik and Sari.

Easygoing delight in their surroundings leads men to pluck hibiscus blooms for decoration as they stride along forest trails.

SAM ABELL

Real and representational, faces of Mbotgate men mirror youth and age, the beginning and end of life. Still-vigorous Miliun gazes on the skull of his father, symbolically fleshed out with clay. His son Galitneman, only about 12 but wearing the wide belt and leaf "nambas" of a male adult, holds his own work: an early effort at crafting the bold features of a clay-and-cobweb mask. It incorporates pig tusks, ceremonial symbols of status, and may represent an ancestor or a spirit.

Lean-to built large enough to shelter the photographer and several men with him in a taro garden demonstrates the manual skills of the Mbotgate and the versatility of one of their favorite raw materials: the leaf. With an informal division of labor, these men take only minutes to complete this rain shelter of overlapping banana leaves. Readily available and waterproof, mature wild taro leaves make a serviceable umbrella. Mbotgate men, with clay pipes obtained via coastal villages, take an efficient and harmonious approach to their jungle resources—a single banana leaf, shaped into a dipper, serves Kamanleever for drinking from a stream. A holder for soft foods like baked taro or yam, the banana leaf may also wrap them for cooking. Kamanlik (below) and Kamanleever wear armbands of bright trade beads; Metakwiri (left and with folded leaf) wears tortoiseshell earrings and clamshell beads from the coast.

Perfectionist in the arts of building weathertight houses in a rainy land, influential and high-ranking elder Miliun adds new lashing to the vine-and-bamboo framework begun by shorts-wearing porters from the coast. To complete this house for the author, Miliun takes the lead in preparing thatch of tangura *leaves for the steep-pitched roof. Constructed with strong and flexible materials, the snug, windowless houses of villages like Yabgatass can withstand constant dampness, occasional tropical storms.*

Overleaf: Relaxed pace of cultivation in a taro garden permits the graceful leisure and conversation the Mbotgate enjoy. When men decide to clear new land and abandon their old plantings, jungle swiftly reclaims both space and sunlight.

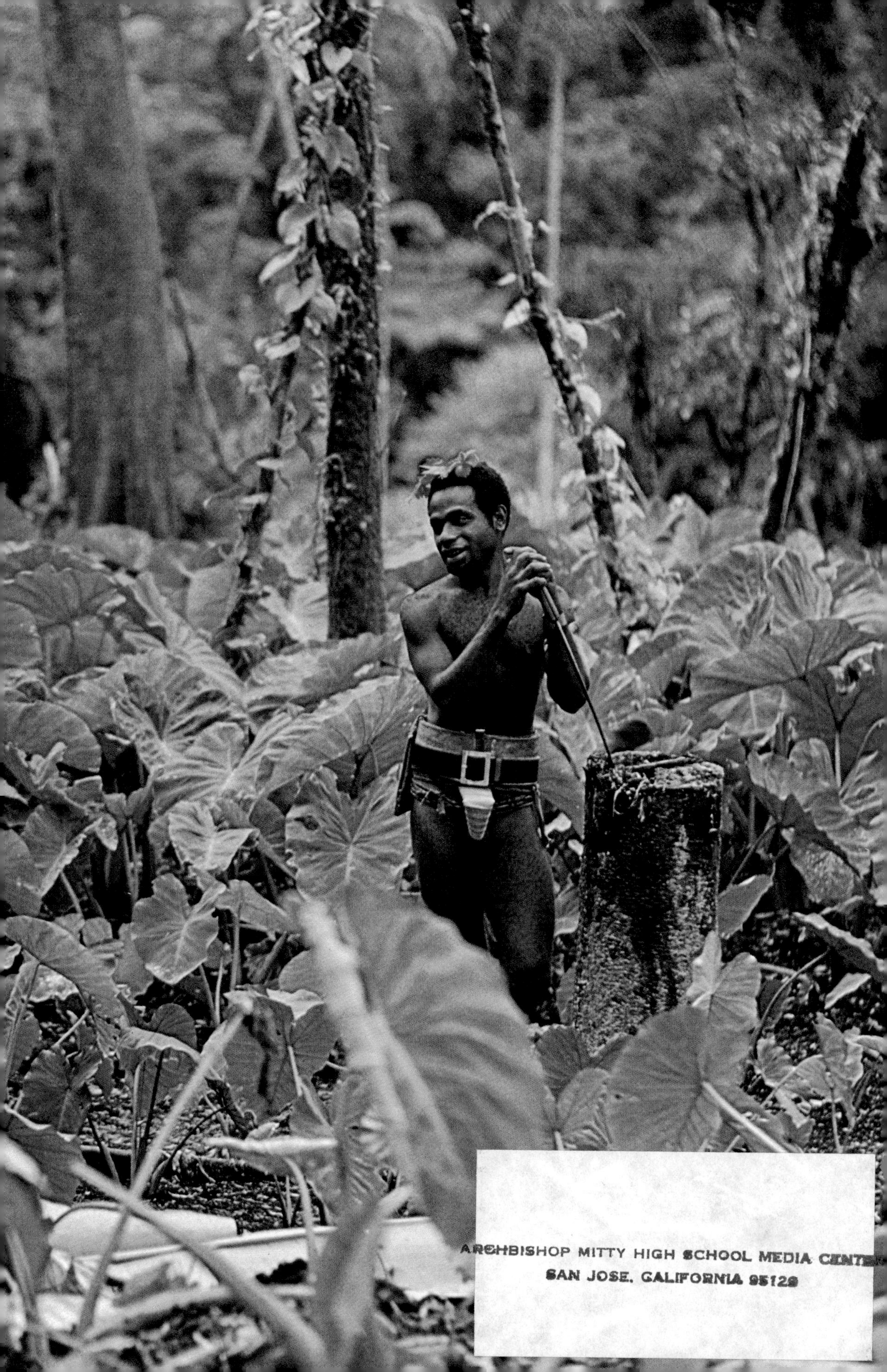

Growing up in Yabgatass emerges as a good-natured round of games and physical warmth and shared interests. Playing "stalk and surprise," boys sharpen skills needed in hunting. At left, Irup cuddles her daughter Legas, who can turn to nearly any adult for comfort. Below, Legas grips a knife used by Mwasak, one of Miliun's wives. Mwasak may have carried her, slung in the long cloth, to a garden—and brought her back, with a full load of firewood and food as well. In almost constant contact with adult activities, children develop confidence and competence from infancy.

E. RICHARD SORENSON

For lunch at a garden, men garnish laplap, *a taro pudding, with edible leaves and flesh from game birds killed on the trail—helpfully plucked by Sari. Because of taboos, men usually attend to their own meals, women cook for themselves and for children. Legas watches Irup revive the fire where she would bake the plantains placed out of reach of a tethered pig, animal of special value.*

Overleaf: While his lunch cooks, Kamanleever savors strong tobacco and rests on a mat of ever-useful banana leaves. Its roof in disrepair but its earth floor still clear, this large unoccupied structure of blackened palm logs stands isolated at a junction of trails.

E. RICHARD SORENSON (BELOW) AND SAM ABELL (INCLUDING OVERLEAF)

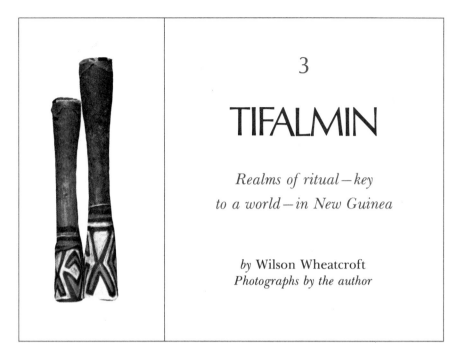

3

TIFALMIN

Realms of ritual — key
to a world — in New Guinea

by Wilson Wheatcroft
Photographs by the author

O MOTHER, you've left us! You used to hunt frogs with us at the river. We laughed together. Now you are to become a ghost!

"O mother, you've left us! You used to garden so well, and grow huge taro. Now your garden will dwindle. Who will make it grow?

"O mother, you've left us!"

Deeply touched, my wife, Peggy, and I tried to be inconspicuous and stood uncomfortably by the door. A dozen women, wailing hysterically, crowded the tiny hut.

The dead woman was lying on her back. Crudely twisted vine ropes bound her wrists. A piece of cane was tightly fixed between wrists and drawn-up knees, lashed thus to keep her in this position as her body stiffened. A younger woman was holding the head of the deceased between her feet; she rocked back and forth slightly as she cried, singing traditional laments with the other women to a spirit departing for the

Wild-boar tusk and cockatoo feathers
give ample ornament to a tribesman
among folk of gentle, sober manner.

invisible village in the nearby mountains. There the spirits of the dead begin another life parallel to this one.

A woman sobbed: "You have been with us all these years. Now you are to become a ghost. You are soon to travel the hidden trail to the abode of the dead."

Peggy and I stepped outside. "They do not mind your presence," our interpreter, Telok, had assured us. And yet we could not help feeling uneasy, wondering if we had intruded on their privacy.

Only a few days before, we had arrived among the Tifalmin to study aspects of religion among this little-known people.

"I am not certain what is proper. Would it be all right if I went into the men's house?" I asked Telok.

"Of course," he responded.

Peggy sat outside the hut where women were mourning and made the acquaintance of two little girls. Telok and I went to the *yowalam,* the men's ceremonial house, at the other end of the village.

The bereaved husband was sitting inside, crying very quietly. He had his back to a dozen of his fellows. His head hung low. Draped over his head and shoulders was a woven net-bag, an emblem of mourning.

The other men greeted me one by one, grasping my extended curved index finger between two of their fingers and suddenly pulling it with a snap. The men did not say much. Puffing tobacco in their long *suuket* cigar holders, they commented with interest on my heavy spiked hiking boots. A couple of men examined them closely, running their fingers over the laces and cleats, then pointing out their discoveries.

I smiled at them, feeling a bit foolish and wondering again if I might be intruding. But apparently life was more or less going on as usual except, I was told, a villager may go to a garden only to harvest food, not to work.

I sat quietly for a while, saying nothing because I was uneasy, but I wondered what had caused the woman's death. Finally, through Telok, I questioned a robust older man with a highly polished pig tusk curving handsomely through his nose.

"Oh," came the casual reply, "she was killed by a *bis* sorcerer."

"What is a bis?" I asked.

"A bis is an evil person who acquires power to kill others by magic. He usually waits in ambush—for a bis will strike only when his victim is alone. Sometimes, though, bis transform themselves into certain game birds, lizards, or toads to lure a hunter or hungry gardener their way. Then they revert to human form to do evil.

"A bis shoots his victim with a magical arrow, robs his body of all its flesh in order to eat it, then stuffs grass or rotten wood in its place. He restores the body to its original appearance and announces the circumstances of death, fixing the time and place. No one ever lives long after encountering a bis! We must always be careful not to be alone, especially when traveling. Anyone in a neighboring parish could be a bis!"

This was the first data I got on sorcery. Now I understood a comment one of the mourning women had made: "She died because her husband quarreled with her often, and consequently left her alone too much." I was pleased with this insight, but fatigued; Telok and I joined Peggy and began our journey home, down a steep trail.

Near the Ilam River we entered the perpetually damp forest with its somewhat pungent odor. Lianas and creepers disappeared up the trees. Dense vegetation just off the trail seemed to choke the earth: ferns, mosses, flowering vines.

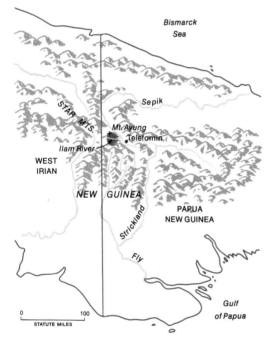

Mountains—and mystery—rim the world of the Tifalmin, whose 13 villages nestle by the Ilam River in the highlands of New Guinea. Some 30 miles west lies the border of Indonesia's province West Irian.

Where the muddy trail entered the open, we could hear the roar of the river, bursting through a narrow gorge after cascading down a 40-foot falls. A crude bridge over the gorge—medium-size fallen trees lashed with vines—shook with every self-conscious step we took. Thirty feet below, the water churned turbulently. Beautiful iridescent blue Ulysses butterflies with black tails occasionally show themselves here, flitting in and out of the breathing shadows into the shifting patches of sunlight.

A ten-minute climb up the other bank forced Peggy and me to stop and rest, while Telok, who never seemed to tire, waited patiently. Winded, we finally arrived at the village where we lived, Bulolengabip—the Village of the Singing Toads.

Ten family houses and three men's houses make up the village, laid out in an oval facing a flat clearing. Only about ten feet square, a family house may shelter four adults and several children. For warmth, each house has a central fireplace, a tiny door, and no windows at all. Near the roof, tar-like soot coats the upper slats in various patterns.

Tifalmin villages are divided into two sections, one exclusively the preserve of initiated males, where men have at least one yowalam in which they display highly sacred relics. The other section of the cleared area, surrounded by family houses, is open to all. Peggy could walk there freely— though if she started to go any distance from the village alone a little girl was sent running to join her as protection against the ever-present bis.

W E HAD INTENDED to live outside the village proper, to give us more privacy and bother the villagers less. But the site we picked, 200 yards from the nearest houses, was just too far away, the old men told us—the bis that roamed at night would surely find an opportunity to attack us. They chose a site only 70 yards distant. In just a few days, with nearly everyone working, they built us a nice house with a traditional grass roof and plaited bamboo walls—and windows. This was our home for almost two years.

Within a few days of our arrival, we had visited all 13 villages of the tribe, some 600 people, living on both sides of the Ilam River near its confluence with the extreme upper Sepik. Closely related in language and culture to more than a dozen other tribes in the area, the Tifalmin live in a grasslands valley about 5,000 feet above sea level, surrounded by beautiful forested mountains.

Like many peoples in isolated jungle-choked pockets on this great island of New Guinea, the Tifalmin know almost nothing of the universe beyond the mountains. Beyond, the world simply ends.

On occasion, from the boundaries of the known, white men emerge in helicopters and planes, laden with strange goods. And in fact we often felt weirdly alien, for the Tifalmin could have no comprehension of our origins or civilization. Strangely costumed, with mysterious powers, we *were* odd, capricious and demanding. Logically enough, they viewed us as quasi-mythical beings somehow connected with Afekan, the supernatural Woman who created Tifalmin culture. How else could they place us in conceptual categories?

To us, their world never lost a beauty and strangeness of its own.

The valley cools off fairly rapidly when the sun goes down, and nearly every night rain falls on the higher slopes. People of the upper valley often wake up in the morning enveloped by surrealistic mist that hovers over the grasslands until the sun comes up over the mountains and melts it away. Loud cries of birds of paradise in the nearby forest drift in the air at dawn, to blend with the occasional whimpering cries of native dogs, the squealing of pigs, and the murmur of rousing people.

The day begins early as the villagers build up the fires that smoldered through the night to keep off the damp chill. Smoke seeps up through the thatched grass rooftops and slowly emerges in delicate patterns. Tifalmin mornings have a peculiar mood all their own.

Few days are not brilliantly sunny by mid-morning. We found the climate almost ideal, the normal temperature fluctuating from the low 60's in early morning to the high 70's in afternoon.

Never a day passed when someone was not peering in at our windows watching me type, or staring in fascination at the rituals Peggy went through preparing meals or washing dishes and clothes.

Even the fact that we washed ourselves amused them during much of our stay, for traditionally they never washed themselves to remove "dirt." Sometimes they washed spiritually contaminating substances from

their bodies, or washed hands heavily soiled from gardening, but this was the extent of it. Every culture defines "dirt" and "being dirty" in different ways, according to complex patterns of adaptation and understanding.

When our neighbors first discovered that our heavy boots concealed soft pinkish feet, they laughed: "Hey! Come look! They have feet like a baby's!" Everybody wanted to touch them. We stared at their callused soles and found the contrast funny ourselves. Often children and the less inhibited adults found themselves stroking our hairy arms and legs with curiosity.

The Tifalmin, who sleep huddled together in the damp chill of night, by choice sit close together as well. This matter-of-fact physical contact was difficult for both Peggy and me to get used to. After some months, however, I no longer minded in the least if an ash-covered, unwashed man lounged against me when we sat talking. Such adaptations became commonplace.

Early in our stay with this gentle-mannered people, I decided one day to go out with several young men who were willing to show me the cave sites where previous generations had often laid their dead. The difficult approach to a nearly inaccessible cliff protected the living from the *sakbal sinik,* ghosts—as did alternative methods like placing the corpse in a tree hollow or tree fork deep in the forest.

We hiked about a mile in shoulder-high grass that scratched and cut our skin. I carried my 16-mm movie tripod; a lad named Agiyok carried other gear.

At one cave I moved a skull to get a better picture. The young men shouted: "*Awaimoo, awaimoo, kerinoo*—That's dangerous, it's taboo, leave them alone!" They stayed below, safe from the spiritually contaminating energy of the bones.

Back in the village, I had an experience that revealed for the first time a major theme of religious life in the tribe. A middle-aged woman named Unonip, one of the wives of Songal, brought her baby when she came to visit Peggy. I reached out to take

With shy propriety, little girls display the feminine dress of all ages: skirts of layered reeds, beads, pounded-bark rain bonnets. For the oldest, a tattoo of soot gives a permanent beauty mark.

the baby, to play with it as I had often done. Abruptly Unonip turned away, insulted, pulling her baby out of reach. She scolded me violently, as if I should know better.

"Don't touch my baby, that's taboo! You've been handling the ancestral bones, so you can't touch my baby for three days—until the *sinik* of the bones leaves you. Otherwise, the sinik will possess my little one, who is small and weak, and its magical force will surely kill him!"

I did not understand this fully. But from related episodes over the months, I began to comprehend this principle of sinik contamination, or magical pollution.

The concept of sinik, or spirit-substance, underlies religion and magic among the Tifalmin. All significant animals (including birds and a few unusual insects), and some trees and smaller plants, have a spiritual component, sinik, a "force" or "power." The invisible sinik of a living or nonliving thing, say the Tifalmin, never exists apart from visible substance. Each substance or animal or plant has its own characteristic sinik, an inseparable part of its nature.

Thus it is sinik that causes danger if an animal is taboo to eat. It is the sinik of sacred objects hidden in the men's ceremonial shrine that makes them taboo to women and children.

Certain things with sinik are harmful upon contact or proximity to nearly everyone in the tribe, causing illness or death. But most substances with sinik endanger either men *or* women. For example, powerful male sinik in the shrine of the yowalam would possess any children or women who came too close. I often heard a father, standing near the shrine, warn his three-year-old not to come too near because it would be magically dangerous.

In exact parallel, men must stay clear of the women's menstrual hut, set apart 20 to 30 feet from the family houses. During her menses a woman must stay in this hut lest she accidentally contaminate an initiated male. Men and women are simply different spiritual beings. This is an obvious aspect of nature.

Late one afternoon, Peggy and I were sitting in Ayapkan's house talking and joking with her and her husband, Yebitok. She was barren, and quite aggressive in manner for a Tifalmin woman, well known for her sharp tongue. Her husband, in contrast, was one of the most easygoing, polite,

and generous men in the tribe. He was an able hunter and gardener, sure of himself, respected by everyone; in the men's house his calm remarks carried weight in decisions affecting the village.

Yebitok was hunched over the fireplace, cooking taro under the hot ashes, turning it now and again with long wooden tongs. He let Ayapkan do most of the talking. The conversation drifted to customs of naming; Ayapkan spoke of her nickname, "Childless." Then, abruptly, she began to question Peggy about a matter that apparently had been on her mind for a long time —difficult questions to ask, socially, but the conversation gave her an opportunity.

THE OTHER WOMEN and I have noticed that though you visit us in the menstrual hut, you never sit there like we have to. And you often wear pants like Wilson does, and have a slim figure like a boy's.

"Further, you do not have any children. We want to know if your physical makeup is truly that of a woman. Or are you something else?"

Peggy and I laughed. "Of course I am a woman. In my country women act differently than you do here. I do not have any children because we do not want any at this time. I have special medicine for this. . . ."

Naturally this perplexed Ayapkan, since she wanted children but could not have any.

In just such incidents we commonly gained insights—through contrasts between the way we saw our world, and the way the Tifalmin saw theirs.

We discovered the full scope of the principle of sinik in numerous, sometimes humorous ways. The men of Bulolengabip often came to us for a piece of newspaper to roll cigars with, a change from the traditional leaf they used. But they refused newsprint with pictures of persons or animals, like comics, because they did not want to inhale such a "person" and become possessed by its sinik. Thus we learned that the word sinik includes the notion of image, or shadow.

The strongest prohibitions concerning sinik warn against eating anything that is taboo—and more than 10 percent of all foods are taboo to somebody—lest one become possessed and fall ill. Logically, in turn, nearly all illness is attributed to sinik possession of one sort or another.

Some years ago when Australian officials introduced the custom of burying the dead, they explained that flies would spread "invisible germs" from the dead to others, making them sick. "To prevent the spread of germs, you must bury your dead!" they ordered the Tifalmin, who still do not understand the germ theory in the least.

But this new rule made sense to them, because it fits in neatly with their own theory of sinik. Even before Western contact, the Tifalmin did not like flies on their food—though they have never been fastidious about it—because flies might carry the sinik of dead bodies they had visited. Someone could easily get sick if he ingested the sinik of the dead on such magically contaminated food.

Like other tribes in the area, the Tifalmin cultivate thick stands of taro in small gardens—a pattern called horticulture. They also cultivate sweet potatoes because the rainfall of 130 inches per year, relatively low for this area of New Guinea, allows it. They grow more than 45 named varieties of taro, 35 of sweet potatoes, 25 of bananas, 20 of sugarcane.

In addition, they cultivate a few of about 25 kinds of edible greens they eat, which supply them with much of their protein. As

Any free moment finds women weaving bilum bags from twisted woody fibers of local trees—and any transaction may include these stretchable open-mesh carryalls as a form of payment.

a tribe they eat more than 225 varieties of birds, marsupials, lizards, frogs, and beetles. Still, they suffer from protein deficiency that affects women more severely than men, and children most of all.

A vast and rigid set of taboos determines who may eat what, on what occasions. These taboos prevent the sinik of certain marsupials and birds from attacking pregnant women, nursing mothers, and young children who are "spiritually weak." In this way the culture deals with the obvious fact of a high infant-mortality rate. Unfortunately this cultural system denies vital protein to those needing it most—and therefore probably contributes to mortality among the youngest. The system is biased to favor men, who (perhaps not incidentally) do most of the hunting.

In gardening, men do the heavy work like clearing the secondary forest of underbrush, stacking and burning it, and cutting light timber and vines or strips of flexible bark to make fences with, as well as planting and harvesting.

Women help clear the underbrush, do some planting and weeding, and much of the harvesting. A simple digging stick, fashioned on the spot, is the most important tool in planting. A hole is made and the taro stalk inserted. A stamp of the foot in the soft earth next to the plant secures it. In six months, the taro root is ready to eat.

Men maintain strong fences around the gardens to keep domestic and wild pigs out. In one day a full-grown pig can devour almost all the tubers in a large sweet-potato garden, eating up months of work. Because taro and sweet potatoes make up about 90 percent of the Tifalmin diet by weight, and because getting enough food is always a serious concern, Tifalmin law takes effect whenever one person's pig breaks into a neighbor's garden. The garden owner typically and justifiably becomes furious.

We were awakened early one morning by shouting interspersed with loud noises from a pig. We ran down to the village. Three irate men were holding a large sow that was squealing horribly. Biok was giving her a lecture in very serious tones:

"Remember that the last time you got in Yebitok's garden we told you not to do it again, and that we would punish you if you went in there a second time. Stupid pig! You ate that garden last night! We are going to cut off one of your front feet so you will remember next time not to root in the gardens."

Blusal brought a log and put it under her right forefoot. The men held her tightly, with her jaws lashed shut, while Yebitok swiftly and neatly cut off the foot with an ax. Released, the sow squealed even louder and hobbled off with surprising speed to hide under her owner's house.

"Why did you do that?" I asked, shocked. "The poor pig may bleed to death!"

"No, she will not die," Yebitok said confidently. "She will be very sad for a few days, but she'll think twice before digging up my garden again!"

Animal husbandry always plays second fiddle to considerations of obligation and retribution. Nevertheless, like New Guinea peoples in general, the Tifalmin do consider their pigs to be the most important living creatures besides humans. They are fond of them, observant of their health, and (within limits) respectful of their likes and dislikes.

Given our Western biases, it surprised us that pigs do not play a more important role as a source of protein. But only on special occasions, such as funerals and other ceremonies, are pigs killed.

Pigs are wealth in themselves. A Tifalmin woman, even a child, can own pigs —forbidden in many New Guinea societies. But gifts and exchanges of pigs are usually business for men: like dealings in shells, tobacco, nubile women, and, recently, money. The donor of a pig acquires not only prestige but credit, and expects a pig in return on some future occasion.

Melanesian societies are notorious for their emphasis on pigs. But the Tifalmin focus their attention on anything they can get to eat—and reports of it. If someone in the parish kills a possum or a wild pig, or harvests many pandanus nuts, for example, rumor about it spreads at once.

Most commonly it was a child who told us of feasts in other villages. One day Folok, a boy of 8, came to my window and eagerly told me, "The people of Yugugubip have just killed a pig."

"Was it a big one?"

"Yes, a big sow."

"Is your family going to get any? And do you think we will get some?"

"My father's sister married a man in that village, so she may give us a little piece. But I don't think we'll get enough to give you any." Discussion always reveals the quality of food, its ownership, and possible avenues of distribution.

The people always act hungry, even though they constantly seem to be chewing on a hunk of baked taro or sweet potato. Perhaps some deficiency gives them continual hunger; or perhaps it is just a cultural pattern always to be ready to receive food.

They express many subtle things—individually and socially—through behavior centered on food, its display and distribution. The generous offering of cooked (and uncooked) food to neighbors and kin symbolizes not only social acceptance but love and concern. Yebitok, one of the most generous people in the parish, once gave away all of a pig except a single small piece. Everyone admired this act extremely.

On the other hand, to beg for a share of available food—*naneng*—is bad manners, characteristic of undisciplined children.

In the constant day-to-day giving and receiving of food, taro carries the most esteem. The word for taro is *ima,* the word used for "food" collectively. Taro is "the best food," "that which makes children grow big." Once when I complained about the tough hike up to the mountain gardens, Taxi, a good-natured lad with the huge thighs typical of the Tifalmin, told me: "You need to eat more taro. We can hike in these mountains without getting tired only because we eat taro."

Almost invariably, when Peggy visited people at home they would offer her taro. Sometimes we had so much in our own garden that she would decline the polite offer—something no one else would do. The villagers accepted this, however, as just another of our strange mannerisms. We did give away produce from our plots as often as we could.

It is rude not to offer food to others. And this assures that if one person or family gets a rather large supply, everyone in that village and many in neighboring villages will share in it.

But precisely because sharing food is a mark of proper behavior, sometimes one must act stealthily to have a supply at all. If a man shoots a bird in the forest, he may

Deep-barbed arrows, thorns lashed to the points, recall a not-too-distant past when the Tifalmin fought with neighbors.

ARROWS APPROXIMATELY 1/4 ACTUAL SIZE

well eat it alone, just to get enough, and not mention the fact until much later so others do not think him stingy.

It astonished us sometimes to observe how small items of food were shared. One morning three little girls found our cat playing with a rat she had just killed. They ran to Peggy: "May we take the rat and cook it for ourselves in your outdoor cook house?" Peggy agreed and started the fire for them. As Kangkan put the rat on the fire to roast it whole, her mother called her. She ran down to the village.

Only about 7, Kangkan was still naive enough to say that a rat was being cooked — women and children began to saunter up to our house. Amused, we wondered how everyone could possibly get a serving. Each morsel went a long way. Through the slow process of cooking and distribution, *eleven* people received several minute pieces, one at a time. (Our cat finally got a taste as well.) Even a child as young as Kangkan knew the basic ethics of food distribution.

After this the children came nearly every morning, usually before we were up, to see if our cat had caught anything. If she had, we gave it to them. But sustaining a balance of food exchange, Tifalmin style, involves amazing responsibilities. Unable to devote all our time to this, we instituted a system of bartering matches or salt or paying with money for local vegetables.

Often adult visitors would pick up a piece of taro to ask who had given or traded it to us. Usually we could not recall precisely who brought that specific hunk. This aspect of our weirdness surprised them in a way that my interest in their ancestors did not.

It is said that in the Beginning, Afekan, the Heroine, the Creatress, lived that she might teach men how to live in strength and dignity. Through her wondrous powers she created the first taro, and pigs, and many items of culture. But at first the pigs were scrawny, and the taro amounted to little. Men were hungry.

Afekan lived with her husband, an ordinary mortal, alone in a small hamlet. But he lived in what would now be called a woman's house, while she lived in a large "men's house." Whenever she killed a wild pig, she threw the skull and jawbones into the bushes.

One day she went hunting, taking her dog. Her husband stayed home, tending the house. She killed many varieties of marsupials, and when she returned she hung her woven net-bag stuffed with them on a tree behind her house. Joining her husband in his small hut, she said: "It is time you learned things and became aware! Tomorrow, kill the fat boar with the huge curled tusks. At night, sleep in my house. I shall stay here. It is time you became aware of the world!"

Early next morning he shot the boar with an arrow, then began to butcher it. Afekan gave him the entire net-bag of game to initiate him into the ways of a hunter. He was delighted beyond belief at such vast quantities of food — never before had he seen so many delicacies! He baked the meat as he had seen her do. He ate more than he had ever done.

Now he began to become aware, and decided to retrieve the pig mandibles and skulls scattered in the bushes. Carefully he installed them on hardwood racks inside his new house. Afekan helped him. They put the mandibles below and the skulls on top, uttering a magical spell: *"Sisilokim kawan bon tima tima!* — May you bring us growth and prosperity!" Then he feasted some more. That night, in their separate houses, they slept better than they ever had.

And before Afekan awoke he made the original discovery of how to make red ceremonial paint. He rubbed it on his face and chest and arms. He went out and stood by the door in the dawn light. When Afekan came forth and saw him — his smooth, scarlet-red skin glistening brightly, new cassowary quills beautifying his nose — she desired him sexually for the first time!

He asked her: "Should I return to the smaller house?"

"No!" she replied. "You have become aware. You must keep this one, and continue to make discoveries on your own. If other men visit you, instruct them in what you have learned."

Ever since that day, men have had secrets from women.

Among the Tifalmin and neighboring tribes, the rites of initiation by which males must pass into manhood are the central experiences of life. They abound in symbolism and mystery. They inspire wonder, and evoke unique states of consciousness.

Before initiation boys are treated symbolically as female. They sleep in the family house, with their mothers. They are not allowed to share the secrets of the men's house, to come too close, or even—

in theory—to wonder what goes on inside.

By the age of puberty, they have invariably passed the first of four common grades of initiation (normally separated by several years). All the initiation ceremonies, *banboomin,* are enormously complex and are broken into ritual phases called *ban.* Purifying the boys from "female" pollutions is a pervasive theme of the first phase and remains important throughout the rest.

The *Kayuban* begins the sequence. Men make elaborate preparations and purify themselves, then isolate the initiates for a day and a night in a family house at the opposite end of the village from the shrine. In this house the boys are no longer "women" but neither are they men. They occupy a social space between the two worlds.

Mothers and sisters pass food to them through open slats above the door. No one may talk with them. Denied water, they are given juicy cucumbers and sugarcane. They must perform natural functions in front of one another, a source of shame. As night wears on, the boys grow nervous, not knowing what to expect come dawn.

In the morning the men kill a ceremonial pig amid hooting and songs to drown its squealing. Women take sticks and beat on the walls of the hut as they sing of their *nalem* possum scratching in a tree hollow, trying to escape. They tell the boys to "scratch" the walls—like the possum, the boys must escape the hunters (the men).

They also sing of nostalgia and gratitude for the boys' help in food gathering all these years, and together they mourn the passage of sons and brothers forever into the world of men!

Once the pig is baked, the men assemble wearing their finest decorations—shells, dog's teeth, feathers, pig tusks—to form a human corridor from the hut to the door of the shrine, and they begin a song urging the boys to enter the shrine, promising better foods. Once initiated, they may eat many "male" foods previously forbidden.

An old man opens the door of the hut and waves long strips of succulent roast pork as the boys emerge. He dangles the meat in their faces, occasionally brushing their lips with it, but does not allow them

Marks of masculine beauty: a plumed bilum bag, hair greased and twisted, a nose ornament of scarab-beetle horns.

even a taste. As the elders sing, he walks slowly backward toward the shrine, leading the boys through a human corridor between social universes.

Before the initiates enter the yowalam, two men slap them with wet *ilon* banana stalks to purify them. A ritual leader smashes a bright-orange ripe cucumber above the door so its juices drip down onto the backs of the boys as they enter—to let the ghosts of the ancestors know that the boys have been sanctified.

INSIDE, men stand front to back, legs apart. They push the boys down to crawl between their open legs from the door to the back of the shrine. This is symbolic birth into manhood; they must suffer shock coming into the world. As they crawl along, the men fiercely grind stinging nettles, *duldul*, into all parts of their bodies. Many of the boys cry as a matter of course.

When I asked Sulukim, a tough individualist known for his wisdom in ritual, why they did this, he replied: "We must hit the boys very hard so they really get stung. If we didn't do this, they wouldn't develop the bodies of men; they wouldn't grow tough and strong. They would just stay weak, like women. Also, the boys have been insolent to us over the years. When we remember this we hit them even harder!"

At the back wall of the shrine the initiates see for the first time the sacred relics they had only heard whispers about before. Men rub their irritated skin with sanctified banana pulp to soothe them.

For womanly sinik has clung to their skin over the years. Ilon juice moistened it outside the shrine; the powerful sinik of nettles brought it to the surface; now it is more thoroughly washed away.

At this sanctified spot the initiates drink a holy potion, juices of roasted pork and marsupial—but the men sing a song that calls it the juice of baked mushrooms. Deception followed by revelation is a characteristic theme of Tifalmin initiations.

Now for the first time the boys are ceremoniously seated on the floor of the shrine as "men" and immediately given generous portions of possum meat, hitherto forbidden them. Influential men explain the significance of the pig mandibles and skulls: magical charms which make the gardens grow. "Your grandfather shot this wild pig up in the mountains behind Fasanabip. He waited patiently at a blind nearly all night and shot it at dawn. Its mandible is very powerful!"

The ghosts of the ancestors feel concern for the bones of pigs they ate and enjoyed. If men respect the relics and keep them holy, the ghosts will be pleased and will make the taro and pigs grow huge. Since taro is "food," the essence of strength, the bones are symbols of life—spiritual life as well as life in this world. The sacred bones are holiness itself!

Later in the day, rites of deception teach morals and proper conduct in the men's house; and in late afternoon a "dead man" covered with pig's blood comes to life to sing and tell the myth of Aganuniyim, a famous character with many humorous difficulties in life—relief from tension that has harrowed the boys since dawn.

Many days of specific rituals follow. The initiates are forced to physical exertion, tricked repeatedly, purified by being burned with hot coals, punished again with nettles, not allowed to sleep, covered with holy red paint and taught how to make it, finally taken to dance at other villages.

Though now they must endure much, later in life men remember the initiation as meaningful beyond any other experience. It dramatizes the mysteries of male symbols, secret myths, and methods of maintaining purity. On the maintenance of purity and the ritual separation of the sexes, the very life of the tribe depends.

Other major ceremonies have different goals and themes. The second, the *Saaminban,* lasts only one day. It changes the spiritual nature of the initiates so they will not be harmed by eating wild pig's flesh.

After the ceremonial hunting and butchering of a wild pig, the initiates are given sanctified pieces of pork mixed with nettles. Deceived into thinking it cooked, they eat it raw—for they are also "raw." Shortly, they are "cooked"—made to lie down on top of the steaming banana-leaf oven where the pig is baking.

Now men flail them with the pig's hide, singing: "Uronokim—Wild Pig of Ritual, Sacred One—you are truly hot, and so are the boys, and so are the boys!" Thrashing the youths with the hide places them "inside the pig," at one with it.

With other symbolic operations, the initiates are thus ritually made into wild pigs. How could the sinik of the wild ones now harm the youths who are their spiritual equals? Being now of one order, the young men shall henceforth be capable of hunting pigs in their own forest-locked domain.

As in the myth when Afekan's husband painted himself red, so today in the third major ceremony a man acquires the beauty necessary to attract a wife.

The most advanced ceremony, the *Amk-unmiitban*, is concerned with the rebuilding of the shrine itself.

While we were living with the Tifalmin, we saw only one modified initiation, although they have reportedly had others since we left in late 1970. The changes toward leniency are due mainly to missionary influence.

WE WITNESSED a remarkable degree of superficial change during our study. I remember how my friend Wansep ran as fast as he could along the trail to Nimnimdubip to fetch a bundle of tobacco and barter it with distant traders for a new palmwood bow and *bonang* shells. When we left, few people were interested in shells; attention had turned now toward money. Australian administration and the Australian Baptist Mission have had the most impact in changing the lives of the Tifalmin.

Most of the tribe, while Christian in name, now stand in both worlds, the traditional and the modern. When the men of Bulolengabip rebuilt the ceremonial shrine, they purified themselves by abstaining from women and water for ten days in advance. But before they took the old shrine apart, Sulukim gave a long Christian prayer.

Still, new ideas—germs, money, God's blessing—remain alien in the world of ghosts and invisible villages, cannibal sorcerers who take the form of neighbors, sinik, magical bones, food taboos. This tapestry of ideas and customs the Tifalmin have woven together constitutes a logical world view, an explanation of their environment, valley and forest and mountain.

How could the Tifalmin understand my world, my research? No one in the tribe, not even my brilliant interpreter Telok, really understood why we had come to live with them and why I was always "fighting the keys of my typing machine." They saw books in our house, and knew that white men "wrote things down in books." But they could not understand why. It was just another of the very strange, powerful things Europeans did.

Many people concluded that in essence we were ancestral ghosts, sakbal sinik, taking the form of white persons in order to visit them again. If we were not, why—unlike any other Europeans—did we come to live among *them*? Why did I always ask about the ancestors, and constantly raise questions about the secret life of the men's-house shrine and the world of ghosts?

Why did we try to learn their language, befriend them, and help them with medicine when they were sick? Why did we have so many powerful things? Wasn't it obvious that we were unpredictable and capricious like ghosts?

These questions puzzled them. Once, sitting quietly in the bachelors' house, several of the old men began to figure out whose father I was the "incarnation" of. They decided I was related to Sulukim, because he was also quite tall.

When we announced our decision to return to our own country, no one could understand why. Had we not been treated well? Had they not given us enough food?

We realized that the only thing they could understand was homesickness, since they often comment on how anxious they are to return home from even a short trading expedition among the mountains. So we told them we were eager to see our families after such a long time. They did understand this.

But a few days after this explanation of our motives, several men came up to our house as a group. They offered to "buy me" from my parents so that we would stay in Bulolengabip. They wanted me to write to my parents on their behalf to ask if they would accept a payment like bride price, so that we could live there permanently.

I had to tell them that Peggy and I must make the decision alone, and that we really did have to leave.

Now, in 1973, the Australian officials are preparing to leave New Guinea, to transfer power to an independent new nation. I wonder what citizenship will mean to the Tifalmin. I remember the question I was sometimes asked in a moment of intimacy, in a resolute effort to understand me and my world: "Come on, tell me! I'm your friend—you can trust me. Are you really a ghost?"

In a posture familiar to Tifalmin mothers, and considered comfortable, a matron nurses her infant at the author's door.

Wandering pig returns home — on the shoulders of two hunters. Although straying, it remained a domestic animal, permissible food for everyone, under the Tifalmin system of taboo. Acting as butchers, Biok (left) and Songal cut the customary stylized incisions with bamboo knives. Then they pile the meat on edible ferns, add vegetables and heated rocks, and cover it all with banana leaves for baking. The pig's owner gives pork to heads of households, who distribute it among their families; as the process begins, children scramble for grease-soaked greens.

Weapons wrapped to signal peace, Tinum Oksapmin tribesmen arrive from West Irian. Traditional trading partners of the Tifalmin, they have journeyed six days through swamp and jungle to bring their products from the lowland forest: hardwood bows and arrow shafts, and pounded-bark capes. At right, Yebitok tests a new black palmwood bow. If it passes inspection, he will trade for it the valued commodity of the highlands, tobacco. The Tifalmin cultivate six varieties, all strong to Western taste. They roll small cigars in moistened leaves of the betelkon *shrub*, and smoke them in long, curved willow holders called suukets.

Following precedent from myth, a man uses a cassowary's leg bone for a knife to cut the inedible white pith from pandanus fruit—the first such fruit grew from the heart of a supernatural hero. Today the seeds, when baked, moistened, and squeezed, give up their oily red coating for a delicacy spread on taro and eaten with a spoon. Nothing so savory goes wasted; women and children suck the discarded pits.

PEGGY WHEATCROFT (BELOW)

PEGGY WHEATCROFT (BELOW)

In the tumbling waters of the Ilam River, women and children search among the rocks for tadpoles. A young girl carries fern-wrapped clay to reinforce a dam built upstream to slow the current; her reed skirt laid aside, she wears a bathing suit of fern fronds for modesty. Women and children, barred by strict taboos from many "male" foods rich in protein, supplement their diets with steamed tadpoles and such roasted snacks as the occasional lizard that a boy corners in the taro garden, large bismanok *spiders, and the tiny* bulolo *toads that give Bulolengabip its lyrical name—Village of the Singing Toads.*

Steady lines of soot trace the geometry of a shield design. Until the 1950's, when Australian administrators brought peace, armed conflict often settled disputes. Tifalmin warriors on foray fought in small groups—one man holding the heavy wooden shield while his archer-companions nocked their arrows to the string. Biok, famed in the tribe for his talents, exhibits three of his finest and most symmetrical designs. He learned his technique from his father. Paint comes from the earth itself: soot, limestone, and iron-rich clay, mixed with juice from a banana stem. Below, a possum's incisor becomes a chisel to carve decorations on the foreshaft of an arrow.

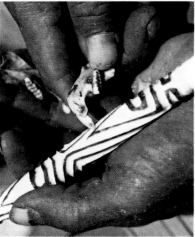

PEGGY WHEATCROFT (OPPOSITE)

Faces covered with sacred red paint, boys prepare to enter the world of men. Drums mark the rhythm as families and friends join them to dance through the village. After complex rites wash away the "female" impurities of childhood, the initiates for the first time may enter the shrine called yowalam. *Here, in this holiest of places, a senior tribesman serves them a sacramental feast of pork and taro, and tells of the magical powers residing in the sacred pig mandibles.*

Overleaf: After daylong feasting, friends gather to share the intimacy of a family house. Shoulder to shoulder at the central baked-clay hearth where firewood dries, they smoke or cuddle a piglet, weave bilum bags, and gossip in peace.

81

4

TURKANA

In a harsh land: a precarious survival, an arduous civility

by Neville Dyson-Hudson
Photographs by Victor Englebert
and the author

"THINK there are rich men and poor men in all places," he said; "that is how God has arranged it." Loceyto wrinkled his forehead, obscuring the four small scars of tribal identity, and his malformed lower lip pushed out as it usually does when he is thinking hard. He wanted the form of his words to clinch the point beyond argument, as rhetoric-conscious Turkana elders always do.

"But *staying* rich—that's the problem. You must drive your children to herd. If you don't watch your sons all the time, they grow idle. They want to be at dances with girls. They want to sing their songs. They just want to play. Then the animals get lost. Or a wealthy man decides he will eat meat all the time. And his people want things. So he sells animals to the Somali traders. He uses up the livestock.

"Soon it's all gone. It's hard to stay rich."

Although we call each other "brother," Loceyto seldom explains his views so ex-

Loceyto, the author's sponsor among the Turkana, proudly wears necklaces that a trader saved for so wealthy a client.

plicitly. But we had come upon his constant concern—keeping enough capital to stay in the game, and keeping the facts of it to himself. Any Swiss banker would see his point of view right away, and approve of it.

After several dry seasons of work on the western flanks of Lake Rudolf, the mystery to me was not how someone could stay rich but how anyone could stay alive in this miserable dust-laden corner of Kenya. When the day comes for a complete official count of people and animals, it will appear that perhaps 200,000 humans and 3,250,000 head of livestock find a livelihood here. But that seems a perpetual miracle.

What meets the eye is black lava outcrops which the erosions of time have reduced to stretches of dull, intimidating rubble; or basement rock ground fine to gravelly sand of evil glint—and all of it, black or white, lying bleak, eroded, inferno-hot to walk upon, even in hide sandals.

Once I stopped in sweating fascination to peer at an insect on a lava outcrop near midday, "the Burning of the Sun." Its legs were absurdly elongated as if to keep its body as far from the rock as possible; and it made ridiculously slow progress because

AKURUM, OR MILK-STORAGE VESSEL; ACTUAL HEIGHT C. 21 INCHES; COURTESY NEVILLE
DYSON-HUDSON; N.G.S. PHOTOGRAPHERS VICTOR R. BOSWELL, JR., AND ROBERT S. OAKES

85

Turkanaland encompasses some 25,000 square miles in northwestern Kenya; the author works south of the Turkwel River. Nomadic herdsmen, the Turkana move every few weeks in the dry season as individual judgment and need for water dictate, less frequently during the rains.

it held up one leg after each complicated move forward, as if cooling one foot at a time on its endless journey.

I wondered if to the eye of Akuj, the Creator, the long-legged Turkana seem to make the same incredible fight for survival. Every few weeks they moved their herds and flocks deliberately across the stony barrens, forever making new shelters of branches and flimsy animal fences of thorn scrub, leaving the old ones to collapse and blow away, as they searched perpetually for scattered grazing and water to keep their animals — and so themselves — alive.

On a good day, I took some pride in trudging through this landscape to do my job: to learn the technique and ecology of herding, and the social patterns that hold a society together when scarcity of resources enforces a resolute competition. On a bad day, the very sight of the terrain made my spirit sink even before a single Turkana turned me away with a curt rebuff.

Although few observers have studied Turkana society, especially in the southern area where I work, they agreed that Turkana were difficult: aloof when not demanding, conservative, truculent.

As I came to understand, Turkana concentrate on the difficult art of existing. For them, outsiders — government officers, missionaries, Somali traders, anthropologists — can neither understand enough nor help enough to justify relaxing an unending wary concern with survival.

Tough, resilient, and antagonistic, the Turkana delighted in putting obstacles in my way. To deal cheerfully with this I needed all the emotional stamina I could get, and the landscape seemed to suck it dry.

In those disappointing first months I kept comparing the Turkana with their cultural cousins the Karimojong on the cooler, greener high plains across the Uganda border, where I had lived happily 17 years before.

The Turkana just didn't come up to standard. They seemed far poorer. The shelters they lived in were scrubbier, as if an extra puff of their country's hot winds would blow them away. The population seemed an odd one: old men, old women, a few middle-aged wives, very small children, and all of them hungry.

For Turkana, in the dry season, hunger is the first, obsessional fact to be communicated: "Blessings! Blessings that we have found each other! Hunger has eaten me —

what is your news?" And their terror fantasy is the witch, *ekapilan,* who prowls ceaselessly by night causing people to die so he may skin them and devour their flesh.

"*Akoro, akoro*—Hunger, hunger, I have hunger," people would say as they came to beg. One hand outstretched and the other pointing to a shrunken belly—drawn into deeper concavity—they seemed willing to parody themselves to convince me.

THE ANIMALS were not as I had expected. Sitting with Loceyto's sons by the befouled green residue of Lokwamozing, a rapidly drying water hole in the central plains, I saw no cattle at all; only a few camels came to drink. Sheep and goats picked their way among the rocks, searching for browse on bushes already stripped bare. Donkeys, their bellies distended by parasites, gave their usual imitation of prosperity in a land where animals, like people, mostly go hungry.

The corrals were every bit as scruffy as the animals themselves. Scrubby thorn branches, barely knee-high, they made a mockery of the sturdy enclosures I'd known with the Karimojong. For camels they were an absurdity. Like an outsize schoolmarm in the chalk circle of a children's game, any camel irritated beyond the bounds of patience, or distracted by outside events, could simply lift its legs and depart.

The ineffectual cries of distress and vain waving of hands with which people followed these dissident animals gave an overwhelming impression of amateur theatricals, badly under-rehearsed. Once at Loceyto's camp I actually sat down in the dust with my head in my hands, muttering, "I don't believe it. I just don't believe it."

Even herding seemed to be beyond the Turkana. Night after night in their camps, a man would appear by the flickering fire, to hold a long conversation with the head of the household before disappearing softly into darkness. Whenever I asked about this, the answer came: "He has lost his camels and wants to know if anyone saw them."

Lost his animals? *Lost* his animals? I felt like a sergeant-major watching a rifle fall from a Guardsman's hand at a royal parade. African herders do *not* lose their animals. . . . I sighed. The Turkana were really not very impressive people.

This glum view amounted to confused perception of a real difference. In several respects the Turkana are unique among eight culturally similar tribes, speaking versions of the same language, clustered at this corner where Kenya, Uganda, Sudan, and Ethiopia meet.

Though language links the Turkana to the people to the west, their tribal scars on the forehead evoke the Nilotic peoples far to the north, and their heavy dependence on camels is shared by tribes to the east. Probably the Turkana have not had much rehearsal time with camels, but acquired them from their eastern neighbors sometime before the present century, beyond the span of living memory.

It took me a long time to stop thinking of Turkana as inferior Karimojong; and if this seems an unpleasant attitude, I would only say that it occurs often enough among anthropologists who have worked in one society and then undertake another. It comes partly from gratitude to individuals who have let you into their lives when, given the differences between you and the trouble in it for them, they could easily have kept you out—as Turkana now seemed determined to exclude me.

But the Turkana used Karimojong comparisons themselves, to place me. Within a week of my arrival I had been named "the Karimojong man" because of my speech.

Cultural cousins these tribes might be, and structural linguists could agree all they liked that the two spoke mutually intelligible dialects. But for all practical purposes I was a bit like a Chinese who has learned his English in Alabama, sent to investigate a village in the Scottish Highlands with the assurance that at least he won't have a language problem.

This frustration was minor compared with that of making entry into the society. To begin to understand Turkana society, which may well contain 10,000 families, I had to find one family that would let me live in their camps until they simply went about their business without reacting to me.

Then I could try to understand what I heard and saw and felt and then, only then, could I begin to trace the threads that link one family to another and another.

It was Loceyto, whatever his motives, who offered his household as people to be with, his homestead as somewhere to visit. His neighbors warned him repeatedly that no good would come of this.

My first visit was a disaster. I had taken gifts: tobacco for him; a 200-pound bag of cornmeal; aluminum cooking pots for four women—three wives and the sister of one, aunt of a mission schoolboy I knew. I distributed the food myself, as if I were head of the household, and in broad daylight at that, so the news spread and people came from miles around to beg.

By giving the food to the women, I left Loceyto with none of it except what he could coax or bully from a wife—for each wife and her children form a unit, and none has the sole responsibility for preparing food for the husband.

Worse, I had given the boy's aunt a share appropriate for a wife; and the other wives complained to Loceyto that one household had gotten a double share. Wrangles of this sort are the plague of a man with more wives than one; Loceyto picked up his tobacco with a growl and went off to chew it in silent rage. That was a short visit.

Loceyto has never introduced me to a wife as such. I know a poor Turkana who carefully explained which of his wives is which; but by telling me about wives and children Loceyto would have told me indirectly about the herds that support them.

Slowly I gained a better footing. I came

Tending calves through the day, a young herder goes armed against the chance of small game for a meal, a prowling hyena—or enemy raiders.

VICTOR ENGLEBERT

to know two of the wives — Abé, cheerfully pugnacious of manner; and Kamusio, a competent household manager but too gentle, I often think, for Turkana society. Loceyto began to tell me, "We are friends. We are really friends. We will help each other." But three months went by before he let me visit a cattle camp. "It is far away," he kept objecting, "in the belly of the mountains." At last he agreed to send me with his younger brother, Ataut, for escort.

In fact the camp lay on the plain, and in late afternoon we found it empty. "You see, they are not here," said Ataut; "we will rest." Turkana are great catnappers. I was excited at my first chance to see a Turkana herding operation from inside: "I haven't come all this way just to rest; let us talk about the cattle."

Like others, Ataut accepted my general interest in cattle as a mark of reason, unusual in a European, but with amusement that I asked so many elementary questions, like a small boy. "At what age do your cows have calves? . . . And how often? . . . How long is a calf suckled? . . . At what age do you castrate the males? . . ."

Loceyto had agreed that I could measure milk yields at the camp, but Ataut grew uneasy when I asked about the size of the herd. (To discuss banking is one thing; to ask for a look at a man's checkbook is something else again.)

"While we wait, tell me the names of the cows whose milk I am to measure." He parried: "You will see them soon." I persisted: "Tell me slowly now so I can write the names in my book." He thought . . . he could see no reason why not: "The Blue One . . . Spear-Horns . . . Redhead . . . Giraffe-Yellow. . . ."

"And another. . . ." "That is all! I forget the others." The least believable of answers. Turkana numerals reach 999, but counting is not the basis for reckoning cattle — you know each beast by name, and Ataut had balked after only a dozen.

Shortly after dark the animals came: calves calling, an occasional jangle of bells. With them came men and herdboys, and the girls who had been handing up troughs of water from wells in a sandy riverbed. A cry: "Who is that with a fire in the camp?" "Ataut — with a visitor, Loceyto's friend the European." "What is a European doing in a camp?" "He has come to see cows milked." "Oh — Europeans." "He has come to measure the milk of the cows!"

"Ehhh" — tones of mild disgust — "Europeans measure everything!"

Warned that "the cows do not know you; they will be frightened if you come close," I sat apart on a small rise of ground, holding my flashlight, notebook, and glass jug calibrated in centimeters.

Girls do the milking, into wooden vessels gripped between the knees (or, with camels, balanced on one knee). Giggling and a bit apprehensive, they would bring the vessel. I poured the milk into the jug — 300 cc's, 650, 480 — wrote down the figure and the cow's name. Somewhat amused at first, the girls finally grew irritated as my work more than doubled the half hour they would normally have taken. A pause.

I called into the dark, "Where is the milk for the next?" "It is finished, all finished," came the answer; "there are no more cows!" I tucked the flashlight between chin and shoulder and leafed back to my notes from Ataut: "Oh? What about the Red One with Only One Horn?"

A feminine chorus of dismay: "O my mother! He knows!" "He knows the names of the cattle!" "How does he know? He has only just come!"

Gloomily Ataut supported me: "Where is the milk of the Black Spotted Cow?"

Whispers, but audible: "Where is it?" "Mixed up with all the other milk, of course." "Show him some — he won't know which cow's it is!" "Tell him . . . tell him, 'yes, that cow is here but the calf got to it so there is no milk left for people!'"

At the next morning's milking the girls — hungry, confused, running shivering from beast to beast in the pre-dawn light — forgot just which names I knew. I caught them out in discrepancies, and recorded more names as well as more figures. By pushing the girls' patience to its absolute limits, I began to get a picture of the herd.

On my three-day visit, I suspect I saw two-thirds of the animals at this camp. Openly counting a herd is atrocious bad manners — and just about impossible anyway, with the beasts jostling about and kicking up dust — and three days is a short time to learn 80-odd animals as individuals. One morning, however, I listed 87 calves, and 62 cows in milk; at a rough average, each gave about a pint at a milking.

Turkana themselves have a measure for milk: *ibole*, the deep cuplike top of the storage vessel called *akurum*. With a consistency surprising for something shaped by eye, an ibole holds almost a quart. Each morning and evening, if possible, a grown man drinks an ibole of milk; I've seen a man empty three or four at one sitting.

By now I have worked out some crude formulas: 2 milch cows will feed a man a day; a single milch camel, or 4 nanny goats or 8 ewes, will feed one man. Of every 100 cows, about 18 will be in milk, so it takes 100 head to support half a dozen men. One man drinks about as much milk as 2 women or 3 to 6 children (who eat more vegetable foods and cornmeal porridge).

Turkana love meat, too, and recognize about 50 cuts. But they can afford to slaughter a cow or camel a few times a year at most. So they eat curds and whey, or butterfat. The hours of shaking milk in a special gourd to produce these foods make a chore for women. Also, women husk and grind poisonous berries which they boil all day to make something edible.

Herdboys, with their bows and arrows, eat anything not big enough to eat them and not fast enough to get away: lizards, birds, ground squirrels, rats, dik-dik, or (with great good luck) gazelle fawns.

Children gather for themselves the fruits and edible roots from a score of trees.

Omnivorous by necessity, the Turkana are the closest thing I know to human vacuum-cleaners. In desperation they even drag their teeth over the unyielding nuts of the doum palm.

It is in this context that a man like Loceyto guards the dimensions of his wealth with something stronger than the average millionaire's zeal. At least once a decade he

Adz flashing, Loceyto's wife Ekali shapes the top for an akurum, *or milk vessel, the classic Turkana art form.*

can expect famine conditions, and more pleas for help than anyone could ever meet. At any time he has complex obligations to his kin, and more appeals than he can reasonably grant. For too long I was less help to him than he expected.

In a land where everyone must push and struggle and hold on, Turkana society ruthlessly distinguishes valid claims from spurious ones. I brought food—good. I had not learned when and how and to whom to lie—bad. I hadn't learned how to refuse a request—even worse.

Guided by misguided generosity, I turned social life into a farce by giving to people Loceyto didn't like, who didn't like him. "My camp is no longer my own!" he lamented. "There're people here I don't even know—and all of them want to beg."

Ignorant of just how far his extended family extended, I sometimes turned away those with a real claim on "his brother"—to his embarrassment and fury.

Considering the chaos I could cause with little information, Loceyto was understandably slow to let me have more. Not until my first rainy-season visit did he allow me to see his other stock camps. I had set out on foot to find him, with hired donkeys and assistants. A late-afternoon downpour caught us on the plain, a cold wind driving rain into our faces; we huddled under a tree until it eased; and finally we took refuge in a tiny day shelter with one of Loceyto's in-laws.

At last I found Loceyto himself, camped at a site called Nadikam, Place of Frothing—that is, where much grass makes the cows prosper and give foaming rich milk. We hugged each other in genuine delight: "Oh, my brother! Oh, my brother!" About a week went by before I raised the question of visiting his cattle camp, and he was unhappy about the idea. I had sent my hired force away and needed donkeys; we wrangled about donkeys for days. As usual, I suspected that he was concealing his wealth and the way he organizes it. "I only want donkeys!" I insisted.

"See—I have donkeys," he announced one day: an ancient male, half-blind; a mare with a foal. I made the mistake of thinking everything was settled.

That night I woke to hear Loceyto ranting up and down with the cry of total exasperation with one's fellow men: "O the Turkana! The Turkana! Do you hear, my brother?" "Yes, you have awakened me; now I hear." "The donkeys are gone!" "Gone? Who could have taken them?" "Why would I be shouting if I knew who had taken them?"

Tethered with old trade rope instead of good Turkana leather, the donkeys had broken away and strayed. I began to suspect a conspiracy, but after a day or two Loceyto produced better ones.

Finally I was ready to set out with two of Loceyto's sons—Itiyen, his troubleshooter and liaison man with dispersed camps; and Ezin of the cheerful grin. With us went Loceyto's unmarried daughter Tyeko, very handsome, very sassy, very spoiled. Her bead necklaces pile up to her proudly lifted chin; her leather cloak always glistens with butterfat; she is greatly indulged. I pity the young man she marries; he won't have her father's resources.

"Very good!" said Loceyto. "And we will escort you all the way to the Somali trading post!" There I could buy food and aluminum pans and cloaks. Turkana men prize imported cotton fabrics and choose them with discrimination. Garish prints are for herdboys; men test the weight of drapery over their arms, and select soft rich hues in the dapple patterns of their world—the markings of animals, the patchy shadows of heavy clouds in strong sun, the spotty shade of branch-made day shelters.

Before we had gone the few miles to the store we had a party of forty. Men came up to walk holding my hand in friendship: "When we get there will there not be sugar?" I parried: "How can there be sugar for all of us?" "But there will be sugar for all Loceyto's relatives, will there not?" "Perhaps." "Yes! And of course there will be tea. For the reason for getting sugar is to have it with the tea."

Strangers joined us: "Blessings! Where are you going?" "With Loceyto's friend—we are going to the store!"

Like an enormous friendly raiding party we swarmed into the store, a clutter of wares under a tent, until the Somalis grew nervous and shouted "Outside! Outside!" I bought sugar and tea—not enough for all—and sandals for a small brother of Itiyen.

And then we forced the pace through the hours of a Turkana day: "the Burning of the Sun"; "Daytime"; "the Decline of the Sun" that begins about 3 p.m. After "the Cooling of the Sun" we made tea at a little spring. Light was fading—from "the Remnants of the Sun" into the dark of "the

Returning"—when, having crossed some 26 miles of plain, we were suddenly in the midst of a camp.

"Who is that?"—a man's voice carried overtones of alarm. "Ezin." "You are here?" "I am here, Lopirakori, and I have brought Nefful who wants to see the cows and measure the milk." "And what does our father say?" "He says of course he may—that's why we are here. And we are very tired and very hungry but Nefful has a little thing that sings songs and when we have had some milk we will hear the songs." By now the family could pronounce my name quite well, though they called my tape recorder *eradi*, radio.

They enjoyed the still-novel experience of hearing themselves sing; I still found novelty in the smoky flavor that marks milk as fresh among the Turkana.

"That's the best milk," women tell you proudly, "the milk you serve to in-laws— in-laws are so critical!" They clean the container by scouring it with small stones, shaken inside with water, and season it by smoking it over a fire. "Otherwise," they say, "it stinks [which is true] and in-laws despise you for being lazy and dirty."

Turkana do not always build night shelters. At this camp the others stretched out on cowhides on the rocky ground. I set up my camp bed and lay under a light blanket and an old army poncho, looking up at the stars; after all, this was a good place to be. Then the biggest, blackest cloud I have ever seen drifted right over me and descended in solid torrents that lasted all night.

Next morning when I talked with Lopirakori, who was running this camp, I knew from the symbolic scar on his right shoulder that he had killed an enemy—one in a raiding party, I learned, that tried to attack his father's herd. He had also proved his skill in good stock management.

Lopirakori's cheerfully ugly face reminds me of his father's; his stocky build fits the name certain western Turkana bear: Zonyoka, Big Bottoms. (Most Turkana look like black Pharaohs, long and skinny of frame, with finely chiseled faces and long noses, used for looking down.)

Balancing a two-gallon water trough, a girl cushions an akurum at her waist; she wears belts of goat's knucklebones.

VICTOR ENGLEBERT

But "Zonyoka" refers primarily to wealth, and is not precisely a compliment. Others say: "The Big Bottoms will do anything for more livestock. They will even marry their daughters to Somalis!"

I had finished my usual irritating work of measuring milk by the time when "the Ground Squirrel Warms Itself" in the sun (about 9 a.m.); and further conversation brought out the fact that Tyeko's older brother Epakan was in charge of "the other camp." *Another* camp?

With that casual remark as a lead, I questioned the brothers until I had a clear account of the herding arrangements at last. Lopirakori was tending the cattle in milk, which get the best grazing available, with five girls for the milking and eight boys for the extra work of guarding calves and building enclosures for them. At a less-favored site Epakan was tending the dry cattle, with a few milch cows for daily food.

Meanwhile Loceyto had kept some milch camels and his small stock (sheep and goats) at Nadikam. He had sent the other camels to a camp in harsher country yet, for camels can survive by browsing on coarse forage where other animals would die.

"We must split up the stock," said Lopirakori succinctly; "there are too many—the grass will be finished too quickly."

But social motives play their part in these herding patterns. Knowledge of who has milk might mean survival in a famine and certainly means reassurance in conditions of uncertainty. Yet a man must conserve his wealth for his family.

Moreover, wealth attracts envy. Others stare at your herd: "You people really must get fat...." Prompted by envy, men may refuse you water at their wells, *ngakare*, as they have the right to do.

In primitive societies, privacy is notoriously close to nonexistent; but men like Loceyto, shifting their animals about and keeping the truth to themselves as far as they can, achieve a kind of privacy of razzle-dazzle. Continually talking poor mouth is one aspect of this.

Thus with my professional questions—"How many animals have you in all? How many females? How many in milk?..."—I was trying to find out precisely what Turkana society is set up to conceal.

In this concealment, I can see, lies a kind of bitter courtesy. Under scarcity truth can be insult. If you turn away a begging neighbor with the words "We have no milk—our bellies are empty also" you at least spare him the implication that he starves by his own lack of skill at herding.

By such means the Turkana manage not to hate each other, and achieve an arduous civility that seldom softens to politeness.

And so, for a long time, it was hard for me to assess Loceyto's wealth, though I learned to scan the herds at the water holes, casually getting a fair count. Sorting out the relationships of his family proved far more difficult, since good manners forbid direct questions on the subject and appearance proved an unreliable guide.

WHILE I still thought that Loceyto had only three wives, I heard from a neighbor that he had a sister in the household also. I cast for this role the oldest-looking woman at his camp, Ekali, still energetic and hard-working. By this time I figured as his brother, not just a friend; as his brother I had to joke with his wives in the cheerfully ribald fashion that Turkana custom decrees for such relatives.

But suggestive humor would be horribly out of place between brother and sister, so whenever Ekali approached I fell silent. At last, one day, she said in a bantering tone: "And what about me? Why do you not joke with me?" Politely I answered with a term of respect: "Ah, old woman, I cannot joke with you, and you know it: only with these young ones, my brother's wives." She stalked away without a word.

Only much later did I realize from an assortment of clues that Ekali was a wife also. In this society my blunder inflicted a special pain: When a woman knows that her husband no longer desires her, she knows also that her children cannot enjoy the favor he shows the offspring of younger women. Before Ekali's younger rivals I had humiliated her grievously. I do not think her son Epakan has forgiven this—my relationship with him remains awkward.

Mothers and children stick together in extended families like this; and the husband's attitude to a wife affects the father's attitude toward her children, while his relationship with those children in turn colors their mother's situation.

Nakutan, Loceyto's senior wife, gauntly carries her age with the dignity of a time-worn monument. A neglected dowager, she stays at a distant camp with her husband's sister; she suffers for the actions of her oldest son, Amadole.

NEVILLE DYSON-HUDSON

Some years ago, Amadole, exercising his right as a married adult, asked his father for a suitable share of livestock and left to herd them elsewhere. At such a moment a Turkana father must face the prospect of old age: Loceyto turns aside from this; he no longer mentions Amadole's name. "Who is he? He is gone. It is finished."

Nakutan's second son, Lopirakori, meets the tensions of this situation with a manner of self-contained indifference. But her next son, Ezin, cannot keep his poise; he quarrels openly with Loceyto.

On a day-to-day basis a grown son has responsibility for managing a herd—dry cattle; milch cattle; camels. But the old man devises strategy, the herds belong to him, sons must come to him for permission to move for new forage and water. He may say, "Yes, move," adding any instructions he likes, or say, "No, stay where you are."

If a son starts to argue, Loceyto gives him a stare like a spearpoint: "Eh! Who is older and who is younger?" "You are older, my father." "And who is herd-owner and who is herdboy?" "You are herd-owner, my father." "Then who knows and who does not know?" "You know, my father." "Then go, and do as you are told."

Pushing matters beyond this is ill-advised for a son in a society dominated by old men. If provoked a father will in effect "demote" a son. So Lomoti, second son of wife number three (Abé), has charge of a camp while Ezin, third son of wife number one (Nakutan), does not. Ezin loses his arguments with Loceyto, of course, and nurses a self-defeating resentment.

Once I did see Itiyen, usually obedient, defy his father over an ostrich feather, smallest of the plumes I had brought Loceyto as a gift. (Turkana men still dress their hair to display these feathers, though the birds are virtually extinct in the region.) Some of the feathers slipped from the plastic wrapping; retrieving them, Itiyen put one in his own headdress, baleful glances from his father notwithstanding. "Put them back," ordered Loceyto.

Bonds of identity with a favorite ox:
A man mimics in dance the curves of its
horns, artificially shaped as they grew;
he notches its ears—"to make it glad,"
Turkana say—when he kills an enemy.

"They are back." "Put them *all* back!" "They *are* all back!" And there the two men stood, looking firmly past each other, until—with a grunt, and a firm grip on the remaining feathers—Loceyto walked away.

And I remember giving Itiyen silver to buy cloaks and tobacco for his father. He squandered most of it on homebrewed liquor at the Lokori trading center and bought trinkets for his fiancée with the rest. But Loceyto was indulgent, and blamed me: "Eh, my brother! What did you do? He is still only a boy. He is not bad. He does not know money. What did you do? It was difficult of you to do that."

THOUGH stark necessity determines many aspects of Turkana life, and custom many others, individuality counts as well. I notice this with Nakutan's daughters: Nangorot and Losio are quiet enough, but Ekitela has all the verbal aggression and resentment of her brother Ezin.

Once as I sat in the wet-season mire of a thorn corral, recording figures on milk yields, Ekitela burst into shrill complaints: "All this way, back and forth, for you to measure. It is too much work. I am tired of it! It is bad!" Tired myself, I snapped back: "You, girl, if you nag like that, no one will want you as a wife. They will call you a mouth-woman!" She went back to the cows, downcast. And I felt sad—if there is any ready way to say "I am sorry" in Turkana, I have not yet discovered it.

Good disposition and good looks count in marriage. I suspect that Kamusio's gentle friendliness makes her Loceyto's favorite wife as well as my favorite "sister-in-law." But of course marriage turns on the all-important question of livestock among the Turkana.

And this adds to Loceyto's responsibilities, drains his resources, diminishes his assets. For each daughter who marries he receives bridewealth, but other members of the family have their share in it. For each son he must not only provide bridewealth to secure a wife, but also give more animals sooner or later as minimal support for a new independent household. When he considers the marriages of daughters and sons in the next few years, he can expect that the "income" of these transactions will not begin to match his expenses.

By now I can estimate his fortune: several hundred cattle, several hundred camels, more than a thousand sheep and goats.

But adding up the individuals in four camps during a recent visit, I find 5 wives, 25 children, 10 other immediate family members, with 27 more distant relatives and dependents: 67 in all. No wonder that he presses a brother's claims on me—for example, to make gifts for Itiyen's wedding—and grows angry if I refuse.

Then, patting his cloak about his well-fleshed frame and glowering at all who seem about to approach him, he strides off to a shady tree in the sandy riverbed nearby. "The men's tree." For men need a shade tree to lie under during the Burning of the Sun, necks on headrests, to chew tobacco and gossip and casually transmit the news—that grass is exhausted at the Blotched Rocks, or water still fairly abundant at the Place of Elephants.

Poorer Turkana in the area sardonically called this "the rich men's tree." Rich men, they said, feel easiest among themselves, and they knew well enough that Loceyto and his cronies were men of fortune.

Belatedly it became clear to me that in Turkana eyes I was the rich man's richer friend. I had talked of my cattle, on my Maryland farm: "Very fat. Red, with a white face." "Ah, that is a handsome animal. And the others?" "They are all like that." But I also told of grass so thick that I cut it and keep it in big shelters for the few bad months. I told of a stream of water that never runs dry.

I have never felt rich; I think I have never been rich—but from being classified as rich, and from lacking wealth enough to meet the needs around me, I finally began to reflect with more sympathy on what Loceyto's problems might be.

Before some of them, his wealth and mine failed. On my second visit, Loceyto himself doled out cornmeal at night in secret, filling each woman's bowls and leather bags. Then, at Ekali's insistence, a small girl was brought for me to inspect: a frightened face; swollen, oozing lids over a badly inflamed eye. "She must go to the hospital right away. I will take her now."

Objections. "I will pay the money. The doctor is very good. Each day I will visit her. When she is well I will bring her again." A refusal. Desperately I tried self-interest: "Look here. If she doesn't go now the eye will die. Who wants a one-eyed wife? Who will take her from you then?" A final, flat refusal. Almost weeping with rage, I gave up and left.

Years later I learned that two days before this, an anxious Loceyto had called in the local *emuron*, or ritual specialist, who had sacrificed a goat, smeared the child with this and that, muttered his incantations. To risk the anger of the emuron for the uncertain promises of a new and alien friend was too much.

But it is the girl herself who reminded me of this: Iwokol, now a full-breasted young woman with a charming smile, who disguises her partial blindness very well. She came up before others to hold my arm gently and say that I had been her friend "from long before, when I was small."

Loceyto himself, in spite of scoffing kin and neighbors, put our developing friendship to an open test one day by arriving with half a dozen curious elders at Lokori, where I was sharing a base camp with other scientists of the Royal Geographical Society South Turkana Expedition.

Regal as an inspecting general, he took a place under a large tree with his companions, waiting to see what welcome they would get. My colleagues and I had a great wooden bowl of porridge prepared, and tea with sugar; and afterward I drove my guests home in a Land-Rover. As we rode along, the old men launched happily into a praise song; and I realized from Loceyto's beaming face that he felt vindicated in a daring gamble.

So, slowly, Turkanaland shows me its own rewards. On foot the land becomes open like the ocean and a man may go in it freely where he will. If the day shelter as a device to keep out rain has all the virtues of a slightly plugged-up colander, it does provide shade and the breeze moves easily through its leafy walls. In the evening I can sit on the floor and wait for the small children to visit, tumbling over each other and chattering; I can watch the women milk camels while a little girl brushes scraps of milk fat from a bowl for her pet puppy.

My brother has come at evening to ask for medicine: "for witches, so I can keep them away. They come by night—just as the Turkana come all day long to see what my brother has brought and beg it from me again, so these come by night to steal my camels and other animals." And I found a capsule of sedative, my own society's antidote for troubles that come by night: "I have medicine for these; not much, but some."

Loceyto and I still perplex each other. I sometimes feel like an indignant Mephistopheles wrongly suspected of wanting a man's wristwatch while I only want his soul.

I wonder why he is so secretive about his wealth, though I see the people who depend on it; he wonders why I want knowledge with such avarice—and neither he nor I can see all those who would share it.

Both of us, I have recognized, are poor. For all his herds, he is poor in peace. The jealousies of co-wives and their children, the collisions of conflicting interests and rights, set animosities swirling around him. His grown sons chafe under his rule—it is galling to be set in authority over a camp, to govern small herdboys, and remain a herdboy still to your father.

Moreover, Loceyto is poor in security. Tomorrow is another predator and another drought and another enemy raid: a life of interminable hazard that can make a mockery of any man's resources.

And I? I have grass and water, I bring silver shillings for Loceyto to pay in tax, but I am poor in knowledge. I have come to share the life of this one family, to respect the Turkana simply as themselves. Soon, perhaps, I can begin to follow the bonds that link Loceyto's family with others—many others, for among the Turkana, each marriage, duly solemnized with a transfer of camels and cattle, makes a new tie with those who did not rank as kindred before, yet another possible source of help when bad times come.

Since my work has only begun and Loceyto's patience has not yet ended, we are due to assist and disappoint, enrage and amuse—and, I hope, understand and forgive—each other many times again. Angry or friendly, we have come to deal with each other not as native and alien, subject and observer, cautious host and intrusive guest, but as one man with another.

If, as I believe, the brotherhood of man is true and possible, no one but a brotherless ninny would assume that it simply means the unaltering peace of tranquillity. By being "brother" to each other, Loceyto and I are, I think, gradually becoming brothers in reality.

Bending to lift a trough, Loceyto's son Itiyen helps his fiancée water his father's flock of sheep and goats at a dry-season well in a riverbed.

VICTOR ENGLEBERT

Hide shields clashing, Turkana men wage a mock battle in a riverbed as friends loudly assess their technique and style. Herding sticks take the place of spears, reserved for neighboring hostile tribes; but men get hurt, even killed, when a stickfight must settle a serious quarrel. In the wet season, when abundant forage lightens the work of herding, friends gather for an alogita, *a tournament of team fights with whips; these combats rarely result in serious injury. Turkana develop fighting skills at an early age: Loceyto's two youngest sons, Logito (left) and Lorion, assail each other with leafy branches; Lorion's sandal made of tire rubber serves as a shield. Female relatives encourage the warriors-to-be; Logito's mother, Ekali (background, right), pulls her hair in amusement. But conflicting claims of inheritance for children of different wives make for tension even in play-fighting.*

VICTOR ENGLEBERT (BELOW) AND NEVILLE DYSON-HUDSON

Loceyto's mixed herd waters daily at troughs filled from ngakare, *wells owned by his social*

group and known by name. Thorn branches keep unwary animals from injuries — and cave-ins.

Profusion of beads and scrap-metal jewelry, important items of trade, indicates wealth and prestige. Itiyen the Elder, a neighbor of Loceyto's, wears an old-fashioned nose ornament of beaten aluminum on ceremonial occasions. His unmarried oldest daughter boasts in the lavish beadwork on her leather cloak the equivalent of a dozen sheep. Presents from Itiyen, her necklaces and those of his seated youngest wife weigh at least ten pounds. Women of rich families or poor decorate their goatskin skirts with narrow rows of beads, sewn with homemade thread of leather. Of a lovely woman, Turkana say: "It's the things she wears that make her beautiful."

ALL, VICTOR ENGLEBERT

Bleak Turkana domain, dotted with acacia trees and thorn scrub, stretches into distant lava hills. Only a few men and animals remain at the encampment, marked by thorn enclosures and round shelters; the rest have resumed the unending search for meager grass and for water during the dry season that lasts from September to April. As the wet season begins, livestock feed eagerly on sweet-scented esegeru, *a spiky herb that briefly carpets the Kailongkol foothills; then they return to the plains. Among lava rock and sand that seem hopelessly barren, notes the author, flowers after rain mark the margin of survival for animals and for their owners.*

*Deftly using her knee as a prop
for the wooden vessel called* elepit,
*Iwokol obtains camel milk, a
mainstay of the meager Turkana
diet. Her mother, Ekali, holds
the animal steady. Loceyto's
youngest wife, Napeyok, attaches
a leather collar to the base
of an akurum. With a smoldering
green branch, Loceyto's daughter
Mama smokes out a pot to disin-
fect it for storing butterfat.
From adolescence women shave
the sides of their heads and
wear the remaining locks in distinctive "rattails" dressed with
a mixture of fat and black earth.*

VICTOR ENGLEBERT (BELOW) AND NEVILLE DYSON-HUDSON

Curved green branches shelter three of Loceyto's children and a visiting neighbor, kinswoman by marriage, at midday. Her pillow an inverted bowl, the woman dozes on a cowhide; the little girl plays with a gazelle horn. The children's haircuts copy livestock brands, marks of clan identity. Above the group hang milk vessels, each individually owned, with storage pots and a leather sack, family property. In late afternoon, Loceyto's senior wife, Nakutan, a grandchild, and her son Ezin rest by the frame of a night shelter; hides will cover it completely after dark. Day or night, each wife has her own shelter, and her younger children sleep in it with her.

VICTOR ENGLEBERT

Only after finishing three hours' work of watering cattle do these young women rest in the

shade with the stock—and only then does one remove painful thorns from her friend's foot.

5

SOMBA

*In the presence of the ancestors,
the time of harvest*

by Victor Englebert
Photographs by the author

MIST like mother-of-pearl hovers over the black earth, paling the sun moon-white. Everywhere smoke rises, for the dry season has come, and the farmers are burning brush from house-plots and fields. Near the flames, like jumping sparks, white egrets snatch locusts on the wing. But it is not smoke that fogs the sky; it is dust blown by the harmattan, a dry wind sweeping off the Sahara from December to February, a wind that has just begun to blow. The rains stopped a month ago and will not resume before April.

The plain, rolling away in gentle waves, ends abruptly at the foot of the Atakora Mountains, which run southwest-northeast. It is punctuated by clusters of trees harboring altars and cemeteries whose sacred character has saved them from the ax of the cultivator. Irregularly dispersed little clay-built castles stand on crests and in depressions, and scattered among them giant baobab trees point tormented

Near their family dwelling, girls pound carob pods in a tree-trunk mortar to produce a strong, mustardlike seasoning.

branches skyward. Together they give a fairy-tale feeling to the landscape.

But the place is real. It is called Kounacogou, and though its houses are scattered over several miles, they belong to kinsmen of one lineage. We are four miles northeast of Boukombé, the large village that is a center of local administration, on the Dahomean side of the Togo-Dahomey border.

Before us spreads a huge mango tree casting a thick shade, reminding me of all the great trees that shelter so many elders' councils in so many parts of Africa. Under the tree people sell millet paste, chickens, and sorghum beer, while others eat and drink and rest, for they have danced away the whole night and the whole morning, and it is now past noon.

Some are still at it. They have formed two concentric circles, the women in the center, the men around them. The women bend low, gripping hoes and making the gestures of cultivation, for this is a dance of harvest. The women wear colorful fabrics wrapped around their waists and the men odd bits and pieces—T-shirts marked "Pittsburgh University" and "Black Power" and "Woodstock," women's blouses, worn for fun. They blow whistles and rattle metal castanets.

They stamp the earth, raising clouds of dust; beads of sweat seep through their velvet-black skins. They divide in two groups, and each—led by a master of improvisation—sings against the other:

"When did you work these last few months?/We only saw you stroll around./ What will you do to eat next year? . . ./ You people, there, of his village,/Will you do nothing about it?"

If the idler is a real person, and usually he is, everybody knows who is meant. The mockery, though good-natured, is a very real discipline that helps the community to control its members. The idler's friends, obliged to defend him, answer:

"How do you know he is lazy?/He does not bother you./His wife has never begged from you./But you have many lazy fellows/ And what are you doing about them?"

The songs follow each other, sarcastic or humorous, ridiculing a bad hunter, or criticizing sons tardy in honoring their father's death—for the Batammaba are ancestor worshipers, and the dead or those about to leave on the long journey back to the ancestors are held in great respect:

"You have no shame, ungrateful sons,/ Leaving your father long without/His funeral ceremony . . ./Will none of you urge his brothers,/Or will you wait a father's vengeance?"

Beside me, my interpreter translates the songs, stealthily following the rhythm. He is also a man of the Batammaba—the name these people give themselves. This is a form of the name used by the men of the Atakora range who speak dialects of the same language, Ditammari. Their Bariba neighbors call the Ditammari-speakers "Somba," and by this name they (and other groups) are now known throughout Dahomey. In this tongue my friend's name, Mpo Tota, means First Son of Sixth Son.

Mpo Tota is a man in transition; he was educated by the French and reared in town. Usually he does laundry for the *Sous-Préfet* who inherited him from a long line of predecessors. Eleven French and five Dahomean administrators have passed him on, apparently with their office. And they have been well served, for he is an intelligent man.

He was, in fact, born the son of a priest, the most important man in his village. But after Mpo received his grammar-school

In the Atakora range and adjacent plain live more than 60,000 people known as "Somba"—a name applied by government officials to members of three ethnic groups who regulate their own society through ties of family, lineage, and clan.

education, his father decided to pass his ritual secrets to a cousin instead. "Now," says Mpo with a trace of bitterness, "I must consult my cousin when I have a problem."

His position in two cultures is fortunate for me, because he talks to me freely about his people as we drive through the wide lands of the Ditammari-speaking Somba—an area of some 2,500 square miles lying around the town of Natitingou and extending into Togo.

The Batammaba probably came to this region from Upper Volta during the 16th and 17th centuries. After driving out the current inhabitants, they found themselves threatened by well-organized, warlike Bariba horsemen. But their fortified houses were easy to defend; the scattered building sites forced the attackers to disperse. The last campaign, a few years before the French took over early in this century, ended in defeat for the Bariba.

The fading sun has dissolved into the sky, and the crowd has gone home. A cool wind cleans the air and little fires nibble at the night. I sit with Mpo and a friend of his, Nda Kwagu (Fourth Son of Third Son), in front of the latter's house.

Because Nda was the youngest son, he stayed at home after his marriage instead of building his own house. This gives parents security in their old age. Now that his father is dead, Nda runs the household, but his eldest brother is head of the family and alone of the sons possesses the secrets of the ancestors' rituals. These secrets are shared, however, by a paternal uncle and, of course, by the head of the lineage—the kinship network that unites several extended families.

In fact, it is the system of kinship and alliance by marriage that knits the Somba together. They do not have—in our political sense—chiefs and rulers.

Nda smokes philosophically as we listen to his two wives quarreling on the terrace above us. His mother has already moved out to a little house of her own, and his first wife may soon follow her.

"Do you have wife problems too?" I ask Mpo. "No, but I married for the second time only a few days ago." "And how did your first wife receive the second one?" "I was married to the second long before my first wife entered the house."

I can only ask for an explanation, and Mpo decides to begin at the beginning: "When I was a boy, my father chose me a wife, a little girl of four. He proposed the marriage to her parents, and when they accepted he went—with a small army of friends and relatives—to help the girl's father cultivate his fields. This my kinsmen did several times a year for ten years.

"At the end of the time, the girl should have been mine, but she preferred another man so I lost her.

"When a man marries a girl without having worked for her, he must give her parents two cows. The French set that fee, but since it is useful and seems fair, we have accepted it. Because the dowry had already been paid in labor, the man had to give the cows to me.

"After some years, what my father had done for me I began doing for myself. I chose a little girl and began working for her father. When this conflicted with my job in town I asked my little brother to take my place and gave him pocket money in return. If I had died, this wife and her children would have become his. The ten years have just elapsed and that is why I got married the other day.

"While I was working for my father-in-law, I met the girl I would marry first but who is legally my second wife. We loved each other from the first, and soon I kidnaped her and brought her home."

Such "abductions," I learned later, are really elopements, permitting a legal marriage by mutual—individual—consent. As Mpo said, he had no reason to make a secret of the matter.

"The people of her village easily found out where she was, and the head of her lineage came to see mine. When my wife refused to go home, I was told to pay two cows to the man who had worked nearly ten years for her. He was angry—understandably—and had it not been for the presence of the elders, we would have fought. Years ago it meant death to pass near the other man's village. Now we only keep away from each other's houses.

"Nevertheless, to avoid situations too hot to handle, you can never steal a girl engaged to a man of your own village."

Next morning we visit another friend of Mpo's called Nduma. We find him resting in the shade of a wooden platform used to dry grain. His wife and the wife of his brother are winnowing millet that their husbands had just finished threshing. When the work is finished, Nduma measures out three small calabashes of grain and hands them to his sister-in-law. Minutes later the two women start winnowing on the sister-in-law's threshing ground.

I ask why Nduma paid the woman if his wife is now helping her. The answer, of course, is that nobody has exactly the same amount of grain to winnow as his neighbor, and it occurs to me that the Batammaba have developed such customs to lessen friction among people who depend so heavily on each other.

Nowhere is this dependence so apparent as in the building of a large house. Almost a castle, the structure is 12 or 14 feet high and more than 30 in diameter. There are several round turrets joined by walls, the whole divided between two floors. The lower half serves for stabling and storage, the upper is partly terrace—used as a work space—plus rooms and granaries in the turrets. A landing between the two stories provides a kitchen during the rainy season.

To the right as one enters stand the altars of the ancestors. The right side is the sacred as well as the men's side of the house. Only the male head of the household may enter the first turret granary on the right, which contains the cereal fonio. The granaries, covered by conical lids, are divided into compartments that hold the staple grains: millet, sorghum, and fonio, and such crops as rice, beans, and peanuts.

Mpo thinks that about 30 percent of Batammaba men know how to build such a house, a *tèkyêtè*. The others must enlist the services of men known to be particularly skilled. But the homeowner-to-be must first cut and carry home the heavy tree trunks for the framework. This is done a year before, to allow the wood to dry; it is then he gives his first party—a banquet copiously wet by *mena,* the ubiquitous and excellent sorghum beer.

When the wood is dry, the claywork begins. Men raise the walls about ten inches and let them dry before shaping the next course. Then they mount the frame and place the ceiling; women fetch water to mix clay—and a second banquet is held.

The final feast is given by the wife (or wives) to women who pack the earth floors and plaster the walls. Thus many hands accomplish a major work.

Grain—wealth itself among the Somba— gleams in the sun as a woman fills bowls with millet, one of several staple crops.

I see that Nduma has greeted one of the passers-by and taken him aside. They sit on the ground, face to face, and Nduma grasps the end of a stick that the man is pointing toward a flat stone placed between them. Nduma is consulting a diviner to find out which of the spirits inhabiting his house is causing him trouble.

THE BATAMMABA believe in one supreme Creator and Master of all things, but their practical dealings are with the spirits of their ancestors, of creatures they have killed, or those that live in earth or stones or trees. God is good, though maybe a little indifferent, so an illness or bad harvest is due to an ancestor who is displeased with them, or perhaps to a monkey or a buffalo they have killed and who now requires propitiating. For this reason, the skulls of animals killed by the head of the household are hung in or near the house until the man himself dies. This permits a diviner to demonstrate which animal is claiming a sacrifice.

The Batammaba believe that the ancestors, the source of their lives, continue to dwell among them. They leave them the ground floor of their houses, and there they erect their altars. Animals stabled there are only eaten at sacrificial feasts and are considered food of the dead. Old people, too weak to climb the stairs every night, sleep downstairs too, and so come closer to the ancestors whom they will soon join.

Nduma is still conferring with the diviner. "Is it the spirit of my deceased grandfather who is angry?" he asks, "or the spirit of my Aunt Nkwa? . . . Some other spirit?" The diviner directs his stick to Nduma's ears, then to his left hand. One of the affronted ancestors was recognizable because of his ears (maybe he was deaf or wore unusual earplugs), another because of his left hand. As Nduma's father is still alive and in good health, he may not have revealed the secrets of the remote ancestors. But the old man will show his son the correct altars on which to make the required sacrifices.

"How does one become a diviner?" I ask.

"One is born a diviner," Mpo answers. "Those chosen by the dead to serve as links between themselves and the living walk often in their sleep during childhood."

"Do the Batammaba consult any other people when they are in trouble?"

"Yes, they go to men who have power to make the spirits speak. They shake a calabash filled with little stones and soon one can hear the spirits speaking faintly but very clearly—and sometimes with great wrath. They can speak any language; I have heard them talk French!"

The day wears toward noon; the atmosphere thickens and the vibrating horizon hypnotizes me. Half dozing, I watch the people disappear one by one into the houses. Only chickens and guinea hens stir about in their constant search for food. Life does not revive until late afternoon when people begin to emerge, and I notice they are all drifting toward the same house. Nduma says an old bachelor is giving a mena party and we are invited.

He is a shy little man, and I wonder if he is trying to buy his neighbors' good will for the time when he can no longer fend for himself. But Mpo says no, he is only obeying the ancient and universal rule: You shall not drink alone.

Mpo and I take many drives through the countryside, and often we see little boys with bows and arrows swinging dead lizards by the tail. "They will grill them and eat them," says Mpo, and adds as if speaking for himself, "but not everyone is fond of lizard meat."

The Batammaba are good hunters but must go to the Togolese part of their domain to find game of any consequence. Here game is rare, though a couple of years ago three elephants wandered into a village near Boukombé. They trampled crops, pushed tree trunks across paths, and went to sleep in front of the houses so people woke up to find their doorways blocked. Fortunately they never hurt anyone, and after three months they simply went away.

Thinking of the danger an archer faces when he hunts really large game, I ask Mpo about arrow poison. He tells me it is made from the seeds of a shrub (Strophanthus) and other wild plants and roots. In fact, when he was a boy he once helped to concoct it.

"I was eleven then and was given the task with three other boys, slightly older. Only children or very old people—or someone willing to avoid sexual relations for three or four months—are allowed to prepare it. An elder gave us the ingredients, and we went to isolate ourselves in a marsh where we spent the night before going to work. We were forbidden to talk to other people.

"We boiled the roots and seeds for hours

and, for good measure, threw in some spiders, scorpions, and viper heads. Then we tried the stuff on a chicken. It died in ten minutes. Had it taken longer, we would have thrown the poison away and started our cookery all over again."

"Vipers! Are there many here?" "Yes," says Mpo soberly, "and they bite many people every year, especially men coming home late after a party.

"Some Batammaba know how to treat snakebite, but they ask for expensive sacrifices—and a lot of beer. And they are not always successful. Now people prefer to go to the dispensary in Boukombé where an injection puts them out of danger. If they get there in time, that is.

"One time a man ran like a lunatic for nearly ten miles and died in horrible convulsions under the windows of the infirmary. Running had only sped the venom to his heart. Generally people try to find someone with a bicycle who will drive them to town on the luggage rack."

The short days pass quickly now. The last farmer has stored his grain; the fields

Set among ancestral altars, a pole bears skulls of animals killed by the head of the family—their spirits may require sacrifice. Beside the door, a shrine honors the place of origin of the lineage.

are empty; the main focus of life has moved elsewhere, for this is the season of leisure and specialization.

Now the hunter hunts, the potter makes pots, the smith forges hoes, axes, and arrowpoints. Animals are easy to see, clay dries better, wounds heal faster. There is time to walk 20 or 25 miles to Natitingou market. And as it is a season of leisure, it is a season of feasts.

After celebrating the harvest, the Batammaba honor their dead, or offer banquets to the families of their promised wives. They also hold initiation ceremonies for the young men and women who have come of age in the past three years. So we do not spend our time with Mpo's friends but cast about for the day's events.

As we drive in the morning with the sun in our eyes, the land looks like an immense silhouette theater. Against the white sky meander long black lines of people carrying all kinds of goods to market on their heads. But one of those black-and-white mornings I remember as red, because on that day Mpo took me to a little mountain village to see how tribal scars are made. The two experts who live there are kept busy during this season. The children brought to them do not come from the plain of Boukombé, where the practice is not followed, but from farther to the east.

When we arrive at nine o'clock the scarifier's assistant is already shaving the forehead of a little girl about four years old. When she gets up she runs to hide her face between her mother's legs. Poor creature! Her own mother puts her down on a bed of leaves and sits over her to keep her from moving. Does she think that the ancestors might take her child in anger if she did not follow their ways? Others come to help, and the operation begins.

Holding a tiny knife, the scarifier squats over the child and starts to make quick, precise, shallow cuts in her face. The tiny knife is as sharp as it is small. While the child screams in terror and pain, blood fills her eyes and mouth. The scarifier puts his thumb in a bowl of murky water, wipes the blood, and continues his work quickly.

Some thirty people, adults and children, sit on a tree trunk nearby and watch. They laugh at the little girl's desperate words, for they have all gone through the operation themselves and have seen many others go through it. I, however, am nauseated and riddled with guilt; I wonder if I am adding to her terror with my camera. I am ready to put it down if she seems to want this. But the curses which make everybody laugh are only directed at her tormentors.

"Why can't you send this horrible man beyond Boukombé?" she screams. "Wait till you let me go and I'll slap each of you!"

Solemn as a hangman, the scarifier is the only one not to laugh. Deeply absorbed, he keeps cutting and wiping the blood. He has the whole face to carve, and the child's suffering lasts so long that even she tires of screaming and only asks dolefully, "How much longer will it take?"

"It will be over soon," her mother says, and after half an hour it does end. When she gets up she does not slap anybody, but goes away hugging her mother, and a bewildered little boy is brought in. Before I can hear the screams of the next little victim, I fill the hands of all the children with candies, and leave.

On Fridays, they hold a tribunal in Boukombé, and visiting it helps me get over the scene I just witnessed. We arrive in time to hear the last two cases.

Three experienced Batammaba elders, well-traveled and literate, sit behind a table to hear the arguments. They pronounce sentence with insight and humor. Impressed by the judges, the table, and its inkpot, the litigants stand before them, scratching their legs and speaking respectfully. The spectators, sitting around on the ground, miss nothing, offer comments, and laugh good-naturedly.

In the first case, the plaintiff—a young man with town clothes and a grammar-school education—accuses a scantily clad country girl of accepting presents from him to the amount of 9,425 francs (about $40) although she now rejects his offer of marriage. He demands complete reimbursement of his expenses.

The girl testifies, then the witnesses, and the audience audibly doubts that any man could spend so much on trivialities for a woman. In the end it appears that he is a clever fellow trying to take advantage of an ignorant girl. The elders decree that she shall repay him about a sixth of the amount he claims.

The second case involves the parents of a girl of 14 and her suitor, a soldier about 20. The father opposes the match and now wants his daughter to marry a former suitor whom he previously had refused. The mother favors the soldier, but the father claims she is prejudiced because the lad comes from her village. Witnesses say the soldier is a good man.

"A free girl must remain free!" shouts someone in the audience. And indeed the girl has the formal status of a free woman since her father never promised her in marriage when she was a child. After conferring, the judges ask the father why he keeps rejecting his daughter's suitors. Does he perhaps want her for himself? They turn to the soldier and say, "Find yourself two cows, young man."

Twice in our outings we come across funeral processions of singing people carrying a corpse wrapped in straw matting. Mpo explains that when a person dies, he is stripped of all ornaments and buried as he was born. Elders have separate graves, but young people are buried with relatives. A woman is returned to her family, for she was only lent to her husband, and babies are buried in a special cemetery because "babies make too much noise."

A year after the death, if the harvest allows—or much longer if the deceased was a young man—a feast is held by the family. Then, if the dead man was an elder, the skulls of the animals he had killed are counted and thrown away.

In this season one sees processions almost every day, and I was able to watch one of primary importance: the pageantry of the *dikuntiri*, the ceremony that confers upon women their full, feminine status.

Preceded by an old priestess and followed by other old women carrying baskets, by singers, and by friends from their villages, the young women advance.

They hold fly whisks and slender lances from which flutter bands of bright-colored cloth; as masculine attributes, these symbolize the achievement of a higher status. The initiates' dark skins set off their ornaments—bands of cowrie shells cross their firm young breasts; many-colored beads swing from their belts; bells hung from neck and arms ring with every step.

Red and white beads designate the woman who has borne a child: a traditional requirement for the dignity of an adult, not always fulfilled in fact.

But the most extraordinary part of the costume is the ritual headdress: a cap shaped like a half eggshell, crowned with a pair of antelope horns and draped with veil-like lengths of gay material.

The women have come to claim food and drink from their husbands to celebrate the great occasion. Before each house the husbands and their families are waiting to receive them. Abruptly the old women stop at one of the houses. They hold out their baskets and demand food. Millet, fonio, yams, tobacco, chickens . . . the old women call for more. Suddenly the crowd bursts out laughing—one of the baskets is filled with baobab fruit, good to eat but without prestige. Someone in the wife's family once insulted one of the husband's relatives, and he is taking a humorous revenge.

At last the old priestess, mistress of the dikuntiri for her clan, leads the wife to the house and places her with her back to the door. At this point the husband could refuse her, saying he has no wife. But this rarely happens.

When the husband accepts his wife, he gives the old priestess a white chicken. She turns the girl around, waves the fowl over her head, and pushes her into the house. Here in privacy the young woman is presented to the ancestors' altars. The white bird, sacrificed to the ancestors, will be eaten by elderly representatives of the two families—for the bonds with the forebears hold as surely as the course of the procession that moves chanting from one house to the next.

The rites of the men's initiation, the *difoni*, will begin in a few weeks, but I must go. I bid farewell to Mpo and hope that one of his Sous-Préfets will finally give him a job worthy of his abilities.

"Never mind," he answers, "the ancestors are the ones who pull the strings. But don't you stay away too long, or you'll find things changed around here."

The harmattan has died. The sun shines like a new gold coin. The great baobabs raise their tormented branches into the clean blue sky; the stubble fields await the women who will sow the grain in spring. In due time the men will share the work of cultivation, the tasks of harvest, and the festivals of the ceremonial year will return with the seasons of the earth.

Women collect millet heads from stalks that men have cut with a knife. For a good crop all thank the ancestors—and no one needs to sing, "Hunger blows his whistle and goes to seek the people. . . ."

Lances and fly whisks, attributes of men, mark the new and higher status of young women marching in procession at their dikuntiri, *or initiation. Now recognized as adults, they may formally join the husbands to whom many were lawfully married in infancy. When a bride enters her husband's house, he stabs an arrow into her head-dress of antelope horns, symbolizing that she comes as a creature taken in the hunt.*

*At her husband's doorway, a bride removes her headdress and the
mistress of the dikuntiri, a ritual specialist for the clan, prepares to
pass a white chicken over her forehead and body before sacrificing
the fowl to the ancestors. Privilege of age gives the priestess men's
ornaments: leather thongs, a basketwork "war helmet" worn under a
calabash for sharing beer. Below, an initiate boasts scar patterns
traditional in the mountains and a quartz lip-jewel of the Boukombé
plain—emblems combined by clans living between these regions.*

Skilled hands shape a clay turret for a tèkyêtè, or Somba dwelling, suitable for half a dozen persons; in fixed order of construction, walls, roof, and granaries will follow. A small—and untypical—enclosure serves as a pigpen. In rooftop work space, peanuts flank sorghum spread on a board; red millet covers a turret, by a parasol bought for prestige; and a man holds a basket of fonio, a cereal now of secondary importance as a food item but still of highest value in myth and ceremony.

Midday heat drives indoors neighbors and kinsmen, members of one lineage. Out of the Sahara blows the harmattan, hazing the distance, blurring the shade of baobab trees, parching the tall stubble of home fields around the scattered houses.

Boys who aspire to become mighty hunters can fashion a toy gun of millet straws—or take their bow and arrows into the bush to shoot real game: lizards they can actually grill and eat. Below, three come home,

successful; above, an alert chameleon, potential victim, balances on a twig. Hunting remains an activity of great interest and prestige; wild quarry worthy of the ancient skills grows rare in Somba country now.

In the year's cycle of duties and festivals, the dry season brings harvest, the threshing and storing of grain, the preparation and enjoyment of feasts. Women at right winnow millet, tossing the threshed grain and fanning away the chaff. Below, men pound fonio, considered most ancient of their cultivated grains, on ground consecrated with the blood of sacrificial oxen. (Women crush all other cereals, using mortars or grinding-stones.) These people will serve fonio at a feast to honor the family of a girl marrying a young man of their kin. Meanwhile, to cheer the toil under the hot sun, a sturdy matron gives the beat, chanting, waving fonio straw, jangling the dancer's bells on her ankles. As the work went on, strong men dropped out and others took their places; but she lasted the whole course.

For every important feast, women of different households cook in the open air, simmering fonio and other grains or highly seasoned sauces over small fires. Sacrifice of a goat or an ox, and the roasting or boiling of meat, take place later, shortly before the actual meal. Feasting confirms good feeling between allied families. And these bonds bring mutual aid in hard times, cooperation at planting and reaping, harmony in the ritual order that shapes all lives, prosperity that proves the ancestors satisfied.

To become a true woman of her people, Somba of the hills, this little four-year-old receives the facial scars whose pattern distinguishes the Batammaba from the group called Besorubè. She lies on a bed of leaves, held by her mother and a friend, while the steady-handed operator incises parallel lines with his tiny scalpel-sharp knife. As the mother winces with her child's pain, small boys edge apprehensively forward, but older spectators, long accustomed to the sight, accept it as that which must be.

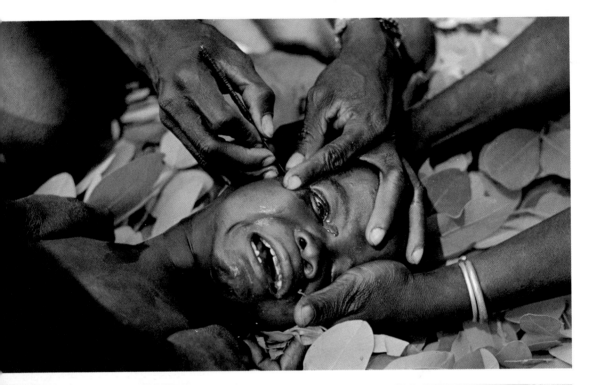

Her ordeal over, the little girl rests on her mother's hip, bloody and tear-stained but reassured. The half-hour operation produces a pattern as finely worked as that of the young man at right, a talented singer. Wearing this helmet trimmed with monkey's hair, he will dance at his initiation, the difoni. Although the Somba have had some contact with Europeans for most of this century, they keep—with flexibility and humor —their own life-sufficing ways. As the anthropologist Paul Mercier puts it, they have learned how "to hold the advantage by being as strange, as inscrutable, as possible. Their traditionalism is action."

6

YĄNOMAMÖ

'Truly of Moon's Blood'—in
peace or war, ever the Fierce People

by Napoleon A. Chagnon
Photographs by the author

A N UNEASY HUSH fell upon us as we saw Kąobawä stop quietly and dart his left arm out as he crouched low. The misty green forest had communicated something to him, something that I, after three years' living with his people, had not yet learned to detect so efficiently. We crept into the shadows, in a semicircle around him.

The dozen of us crouched and listened intently, scanning the silent jungle. My companions clutched their bows and arrows at the ready, and I my shotgun. A younger man whispered anxiously: "They'll kill us! Let's turn back before they know we're here!"

Only the raucous cry of the black *kobari* bird broke the intensifying silence, but it warned even me of human presence.

Whose? Uncertain friends, or sworn enemies? We strained harder to hear what Kąobawä, the headman, had detected a few critical moments earlier: human voices, now faint, somewhere in the gray shadows

Warrior-diplomat, awaiting envoys
of a hostile village, wears buzzard
down in his hair to signify good will.

ahead. Glancing around, I thought about the small, but significant, edge this headman holds over those who walk behind him on these trails in Venezuelan jungle. I felt a sense of awe that I was privileged to travel in such competent company and to feel a part of something millennia old.

I cherish these exciting and precarious moments, for they link me to my own ancestors who also walked in trackless history, somewhere, sometime, in Eurasia.

I work among the Yąnomamö: the Fierce People, they call themselves with pride—and with justice. Some 10,000 in number, they live in villages scattered through 42,000 square miles of tropical forest. With fewer than 40 inhabitants, a village cannot hold off its enemies; with more than 250, it cannot long sustain internal peace.

Here jealous quarrels set brother against brother. Fierceness does not flare into blood feuds, one family united against another. Instead, chronic warfare pits village against village, kinsmen against kinsmen. People and their village go by one name—"We are Bisaasi-teri," say those who live there.

Only the most able become leaders, men

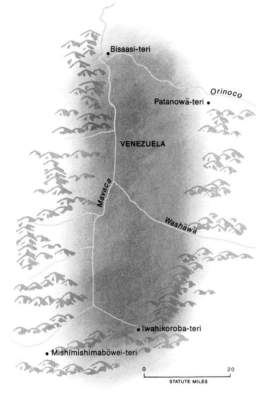

In the heart of Yąnomamö country, warfare among co-tribesmen limits village sites: at least two days' march from enemy settlements. Some 10,000 Yąnomamö live at gardens scattered over 42,000 square miles in Venezuela and northern Brazil.

as gifted as my wise friend Kąobawä. Steady of manner and stalwart in build, prudent and intense, he established his reputation for ferocity years ago. In his village he has secured the status of headman—literally, "one who *really* lives here."

In company like this I hope to learn what my own past was like, when I walk in one of the few places where men still live by unaltered tribal ways: on a desolate trail somewhere near the headwaters of the Orinoco River in southern Venezuela.

Kąobawä knew this area well, for he had led his raiders through it many times, exacting vengeance on hostile co-tribesmen for their offenses against Bisaasi-teri. Two villages stood nearby. One he intended to visit now, hoping to establish peace. The other he would never see, unless it were down the shaft of his war arrow; against that group, the Iwahikoroba-teri, his enmity would never cease. He had sworn this to me. All of his companions had lost close relatives in the wars with that group, and in turn had taken a heavy toll on them.

In some respects, I knew this area better than Kąobawä did, from my annual fieldwork here. I had come to know the 275 people of the strong village of Mishimishimaböwei-teri, our destination. When their leaders had offered to make peace with Kąobawä, ending a war twenty years long, I had vouched for their sincerity. And my friends among them had told me rumors....

The Iwahikoroba-teri had vowed to kill me on sight. I was friendly with their enemies, they said; I failed to bring them gifts; I practiced harmful magic against them. I had not yet seen any of my accusers, I might meet them by accident now.

Droplets of cold water fell on our naked skin as we wiggled more deeply into the shelter of rain-moistened leaves. Whoever were ahead of us, we held our ground as they came closer.

Then I recognized one of the voices—a man from Mishimishimaböwei-teri. I whispered this bit of reassurance to Kąobawä: "It's Yarabiawä!" He whispered back: "Is he Wadoshewä's younger brother?"

The genealogies I had spent years collecting whirred through my mind. In encounters like this, accuracy comes into its own. "Yes! That's the one, that's him! He is also a brother to Daramasiwä, another big wheel in the village!"

Kąobawä stood up slowly, put his cupped hands to his mouth, and shouted: "Brother-in-law! I have come with my brothers to visit you! I am Bisaasi-teri. My nephew Shaki is with us! We have come to visit in peace!" I felt honored that he should bother to mention my name (in a version that suits Yąnomamö tongues) and give me the status of visiting dignitary.

Silence hung ominously over the forest; even the kobari birds ceased their shrill calls. As it lingered, I thought uneasily about my role in this meeting, for I had encouraged Kąobawä to face its risks.

Still not visible, Yarabiawä broke the silence: "Shaki! Is it you? Do you have Bisaasi-teri with you? Are you many?"

At this I relaxed and stood up: "Yes! My brother-in-law, it is truly me. I have Bisa-asi-teri with me, including my uncle, the one who really lives there in that village! We are almost many!"

THEN the forest erupted with the characteristic Yąnomamö greeting, friendly and exuberant: "Aooooo! Aaaoo! Aaaoo!" And they came rushing toward us, a score of them, ostentatiously keeping their bows and arrows down so as not to alarm us.

They had not seen me in a year. Quickly, in turn, they greeted me, dutifully commenting on the magnificence of my red *ara* feathers and the turkey scalps I wore on my arms. But since early childhood they had never seen Kąobawä and his brothers —in friendly circumstances.

My companions, all the prominent men of Kąobawä's village, were standing there with weapons gripped upright, bow and arrows together at the vertical, in the formal pose of visitors. They stared into space, displaying their feathers and red *nara* paint, strutting as it were while perfectly motionless. Only a quivering at the lips betrayed their suspense as men approached to admire their finery: "Aaaoo! Aaaoo! Aaaoo! Look how beautiful this one is! Look at his *werehi* feathers! Isn't he beautiful in them! Aaoo!"

The visitors remained silent and stood unflinchingly for the examination, as propriety demands. For all, the situation was charged with intensity and anxiety, but the formal enthusiasm cut through it and, while nervous, everyone knew what to do and did it with exaggerated dignity and care.

Yarabiawä, some 25 years old, was the most senior of this party of young hunters —a political nobody in his village, though a member of one of the larger and most significant lineages there. He ordered the others of his scant party to make us comfortable. They had their vine hammocks with them and bade us rest. "Quickly!" shouted Yarabiawä to several nervous youths. "You! Go fetch some *yei* fruits over there! You! Make a container and bring water from that stream!"

The young men dashed off into the jungle while we took up formal reclining poses in the small hammocks, one hand supporting the head. Yarabiawä dropped to his knees, unstrung his bow, and began digging a hole in the clay with the end of it, jabbering courtesies as he worked, assuring the visitors that everybody would be delighted to welcome them.

I noticed, however, that lips still trembled with uncertainty, for both parties were suspicious, even terrified. The last time they had seen each other they were killing from ambush.

Yarabiawä quickly lined the shallow pit with leaves. By then the others were returning hastily with leaf bundles of palm fruits, dropping them at his side. He opened the packages and set upon the fruits with strong jaws, breaking open the rind and spitting the sweet, slimy seeds into the pit. Others dumped water into it from leaf containers until it was filled. Then he plunged both hands into it and began squeezing and kneading the seeds until they yielded their milky, pungent juice for a delicious beverage. He ordered the others to make cups out of leaves; this done, he began serving us. He took the first cup to Kąobawä, whom he had recognized at once as the leader of our party.

Out of nothing and with no warning Yarabiawä had created a repast fit for any visiting dignitary, and the jungle had yielded another of its unexpected products: a summit meeting complete with banquet.

Mishimishimaböwei-teri was still several hours away. It was growing dark, so we camped where we were. Yarabiawä sent one of his party off at a trot to announce our coming, and we retired. No one could overlook the chance of treachery; only pride controlled a profound apprehension.

We were up at dawn and soon on the trail. Yarabiawä and the others led the way; I followed them leading my "fathers-in-law"—an honor Kąobawä frequently relinquished to me when we visited distant villages.

When I address Kąobawä as *shoabe*—the

affectionate term used with a father-in-law, a grandfather, or a mother's brother — I do so because this sets our relationship on the best possible footing. It implies a greater deference on my part than other terms would. Among the Yąnomamö, I always use kinship terms. There are no other terms of courtesy.

Yet kinship alone does not always determine an identity. The people of Mishimishimaböwei-teri and a dozen other villages are called the "Shamatari" by their nearest neighbors, and this name has political overtones. If I had to distinguish this group from other Yąnomamö, I would call them the Fiercer People.

Although Yarabiawä's cordiality had blunted the edge of anxiety, and although the sun was high, I noticed a chill of nervousness fall over my comrades as we stood outside Mishimishimaböwei-teri at last. Quietly we prepared our decorations.

We were about to meet the real political powers of the village: the youthful Möawä, proud and extraordinarily fierce, whose father had been treacherously killed by Kąobawä's people; and Wadoshewä, Yarabiawä's older brother. Wadoshewä still limped from an ancient arrow wound in the pelvis — an arrow that Kąobawä himself shot during that treacherous feast in 1950, a feast at which Kąobawä's own father was mortally wounded by these hosts awaiting us now.

We took the last yards of trail past the felled trees of an immense garden. We reached the clearing where the great *shabono,* a circular pole-and-thatch structure of close-set houses, surrounds a central plaza open to the sky.

Whistling sharply to announce our arrival, we marched proudly into the huge

Blackened with charcoal, a sign of imminent battle or a symbol of threat, a warrior checks his weapons. The waiteri, *the fierce people, have built a way of life based on aggression — and devised rituals intended to control it.*

village in a roar of greetings. We strutted silently to the middle of the plaza and took up the visitor's pose once again. At such moments a villager may catch up his bow and cut a stranger down; it has happened. We were surrounded by scores of men who shouted and shook their weapons menacingly at us—a formal intimidation for all visitors. The more enthusiastic the display, the warmer the welcome: "Aaaoo! Aaaooo! Aaaooo!"

Out of the corner of my eye I could see Möawä at his house, observing us intently. Men dashed in at us, aiming arrows at our faces, dashed away and ecstatically rattled the arrows over their heads, prancing and whirling. "Aoooo! Aaaoo! Aaaoo!"

After a long time we were invited to Möawä's house. We reclined in hammocks while our hosts served hot banana soup, peach-palm fruits, and smoked wild turkey.

As we finished our meal, eating ravenously and conspicuously to show our appreciation, the mature men moved in closer and the inevitable monologues began. Kąobawä rose to his feet while his brothers left their hammocks and squatted around him, listening intently. Möawä and his men surrounded them, also squatting.

Kąobawä, as the one who really lived in Bisaasi-teri, began: "Yes! It was really Husiwä of our group who wanted us to attack your people. He erroneously believed the rumors that you were practicing harmful magic against us—attempting to kill our children by sending *hekura* spirits to devour their souls.

"That is why some of us raided you in the past and killed many Shamatari people, but not those of your group!"

Men of both parties clicked their tongues in approval and slapped their thighs with their hands, rocking back and forth rhythmically from one foot to the other.

Möawä, as the one who really lived in Mishimishimaböwei-teri, then replied: "Ahhh! It is true as you speak of it! In revenge, we listened to those in Iwahikoroba-teri, to their plea that we should invite you to a feast and set upon you with our bow-staves. We listened, and we invited you to our village.

"But they were the ones—the true Shamatari—who did all the killing, not us! It was the Shamatari! They are now living elsewhere, because we cannot tolerate them!

"Brother-in-law! Is this not the truth? We were, even then, your true friends and some of us helped you escape the killing by breaking holes in the palisade!

"Again, it was the Shamatari who invited your other enemies to lie in ambush and shoot you when you fled the killing inside!"

More tongue-clicking and "Aaaahhhs" from the intently listening men, whose lower lips protruded from enormous wads of fresh chewing tobacco.

Kąobawä rose again, magnanimous and sagacious, and spoke to Möawä: "Yes, brother-in-law! You speak the truth! It was the treachery of the Shamatari, and you certainly are not one of them! They indeed live elsewhere now!"

A chorus of approving "Ahhhhs," and they exchanged roles again, speaking brilliantly and effectively about the less sordid details of the past.

I smiled to myself, for both were denying in public what they had privately assured me is the truth. But only by such extravagant public manipulations of events could war slip imperceptibly into an uneasy peace—for a day, a week, a year?

War comes easy to the Yąnomamö but peace must be actively and ambitiously wrought from many things: from their unpretentious kinship and marriage system, their trading, their feasting. It rests on their willingness to help each other raid enemies, or offer refuge to allies driven away from their gardens, their source of livelihood.

As the diplomats' speeches continued, I quietly picked up my fieldbooks and slipped unobtrusively between the red nara-smeared bodies toward Dedeheiwä, a remarkable old man full three score and ten years of age, graying at the beard, a fount of knowledge and wisdom such as I have only encountered rarely in either his or my own culture.

Dedeheiwä is one of my courts of last resort when I must verify conflicting genealogical accounts given by other informants elsewhere. The historian, consulting his books and parchments, must understand the family links of dynasties; I must understand the ties among all these villagers, as known to living memory. Having no written language, Dedeheiwä must retain all information in his head; and when men must do that, they can justly claim, as he does, "I *possess* the truth."

Here, as elsewhere, knowledge is power and power is status.

He is a dignified man, proud and confident of his superior wisdom, a man who would not have been out of place in a triumphal chariot at Rome, or borne in a litter through the flower-strewn streets of Imperial Cuzco, the Inca, Son of the Sun.

Here, in his own society, though a son of Moon, he is only first among equals, the most senior competent man of his patrilineal kinship group. A quirk of history confines his talents to giving his sisters and daughters in marriage to other powerful kinship groups within his village, forging shaky alliances among close relatives.

Born in a different era and in a different society, Dedeheiwä might have crossed the Alps with elephants, or extended his conquests as far as Alexander's. His son-in-law Möawä would have outdone even him in the right circumstances.

Möawä is truly man defined as a political animal. He carries the fierce ideals of his culture to their farthest extremes. He combines skill, force, and poise so efficiently that he was able to expel from his group the experienced leaders of his father's generation—and yet keep most of their followers in his own village.

Like all Yąnomamö headmen, he must constantly order what everybody will probably do anyway, for he cannot risk his status by giving a public command that will be disobeyed. Unlike most, he seems to experiment with power; he turns any social situation into a display of authority.

To me, kings, emperors, and headmen seem everywhere interchangeable. They aspire to high position, not by genius unalloyed, but within a certain culture. The primitive world has undoubtedly had its share of men who could have filled history books with great and lasting achievements.

A primitive society accords status to any who aspire to it and make good their aspiration. Thereby it generates competence. In historic societies most men know they can never lead because they were born the seventh son, or of the wrong group, or without wealth. Such knowledge depresses enthusiasm . . . and often those who lead have come to power for reasons other than sheer competence.

But historic societies can afford a measure of incompetence—the power of their leaders resides in the office, not in the leader alone. The primitive world consistently has competent leaders—they *are* the office and make of it what they will.

So Kąobawä is leader by virtue of self-command, Möawä by ruthless will, Dedeheiwä by spiritual authority—all, by insight; all, by achievement.

"Come! Brother-in-law!" I spoke softly to Dedeheiwä. "Let us go to the garden. Let's work there alone!" He looked up quickly, thought a moment, and grunted his approval. We slipped out of the crowd and walked quietly to his garden. There we could begin reviewing the long lists of genealogical relationships bound neatly in my computer printout book: the names of nearly 10,000 Yąnomamö living and dead, from some 50 villages.

About 6,000 came from distant communities, villages unknown even to Dedeheiwä. The other 4,000 names would carry significance to him—including individuals who live four or five villages away or who lived several generations ago. He possesses these truths.

We passed several groups of women, trudging slowly and pigeon-toed under enormous basketloads of firewood, returning in the late afternoon sun to their households to prepare the evening meal.

A cool, damp silence was falling on the forested hills that surrounded the village. So vast is the forest that the pitiful clearings made by men who plant their crops among the felled, charred timbers seemed incongruent with the Yąnomamö conviction that men are Domestic because they have gardens, and all else is Feral.

Culture and Nature are sharply held apart in Yąnomamö beliefs, in spite of what would appear to be insuperable odds. The jungle—Urihi—is overwhelming, set against the portion of it men have claimed from Nature. Yet beyond its vastness the Yąnomamö define a rich and ordered universe.

Urihi stretches from the Layer of the Upper Heavens to the Lower, home eternally of the departed, whence the sun comes and whither it goes before doubling back under This Layer, where mortals dwell. It re-emerges at dawn and retraces the course of the moon, endlessly, as it was when the First Beings lived, when one of them shot Moon with his arrow and Moon's blood fell to This Layer and formed the first human beings—Yąnomamö. Born in blood, Men were born to be Fierce.

Thus it was in the beginning, yesterday or forever, and shall ever be. Time's arrow has no point, no course. Each present moment is the center of ripples from a pebble dropped into a calm pool. Yąnomamö history lacks the long and eerie transience of a river.

At the edge of Dedeheiwä's garden, Nature began and Culture ended. We straddled a large, damp log and began going over the questions I had prepared.

I quickly rechecked to see if any referred to his deceased close relatives. Back in Ann Arbor, Michigan, I had run a yellow line through all those names I could not speak in his presence, names that would cause him sadness or anguish. Respect reaching the intensity of dread limits the use of names among the Yąnomamö. A name spoken at the wrong moment can provoke desperate distress—or rage.

I switched on my tape recorder and began to read awe-inspiring names. All have their value in explaining this society. I had recorded them and reduced them to writing, for I could not hope to "possess" so much truth myself. Dedeheiwä often chided me because my "leaves" (my papers) possessed more truth than I did.

When men say "father" and "brother" out of courtesy, an outsider often finds confusion: I asked him if a man named Paredowä was "the real father of Momowä." Dedeheiwä winced at Momowä's name, for this was a distant kinsman, long dead.

He looked nervously around, grabbed me by the head, pulled me roughly toward him. In the hissing tones of excitement, he whispered: "That was *not* Paredowä! The Aramamisi-teri shot *him* full of arrows before I was born, in revenge for an earlier killing. It happened long ago, at the time when Moon's blood fell to This Layer. Momowä was truly of Moon's blood!"

He asked me to look through my leaves for the name he had given me several years earlier, and I quoted it softly.

"Ahhh! Yes! Yes! That's the one! That's him! Why didn't you believe me in the first place?"

I blushed, and admitted my "foolish mistake." I checked my tape recorder. I made certain that the speaker was disengaged so I would not inadvertently blare the secrets of my craft into the garden or, worse yet, the village. I had been chased around villages before, by infuriated men with clubs or firebrands, for speaking the name of someone whose death I had not known of.

I continued. "I am confused about the

father of Moshiwariwä, who lives in your village. Who is Moshiwariwä's father, the one who truly sired him?"

Dedeheiwä's face turned ashen. "Don't! Stop! Don't ask that!" He glanced around anxiously and whispered, ever so softly: "Brother-in-law! It is good that nobody heard you! His father was the very one who also sired my daughter's husband, the one that a man of Kạobawä's group killed at Patanowä garden with his ax! He was the father of *the one who really lives here!* Do not ask further about him!"

Möawä's father!

I became suddenly weak, for I might have put my companions in serious danger. I had blundered onto the touchiest grievance of the village's strongest, most quick-tempered headman. Kạobawä had risked this visit to draw attention away from a past filled with bloodshed and anguish; the wary and poetic speeches going on in the shabono were devoted to that end.

Yet I, whose paper possessed more truth than my head, clumsily stumbled through my leaves and wandered into social thickets that three years' experience had not yet made visible enough to me. I acknowledged it. At least I had learned to choose the remoteness of the garden.

We worked for two hours, correcting and updating information. Slowly the

Uneasy among traditional enemies,
a youth makes a gesture of peace
by accepting soup from a gourd cup.

history and genealogical data of a dozen villages showed a pattern that all informants would agree upon.

I also saw just how many adult men of Mishimishimaböwei-teri shared deep grievances against Kąobawä and his brothers. In twenty years children had grown into manhood; probably Kąobawä himself did not know how many belonged to his adversaries' group.

It grew cooler and Dedeheiwä began rubbing his arms. "Shaki! Raiders travel at night!" He was teasing me. "Yes, I know. Let's go back to the village."

It was nearly dark when we walked quietly across the plaza. The shabono's huge arc was dotted every few feet with dancing fires, thin wisps of blue smoke rising along the inclined roof and filtering through the palm fringes at its edge.

Kąobawä and his brothers had spent much of the afternoon with people they had not visited for two decades. Elaborate promises were made to give dogs, bows, arrows, baskets, hallucinogenic snuff, tobacco, cotton yarn and cotton hammocks.

Best of all, the visitors promised their hosts machetes. Bisaasi-teri now had foreigners living in it, people who brought machetes and talked only of their Spirit — they came from God's village.

A shaman himself, Möawä had no use for missionaries and their "hekura." To him the new source of machetes was all-important. Machetes reached his village only through long and variable trade routes; they arrived badly worn or broken.

With machetes, gardens could be cleared relatively easily. A few machetes or pieces of broken steel had trickled into his village before his day — even back in the time of Moon Blood, from many miles away, by trade networks involving other tribes, other foreigners. Before that, men cleared gardens only with fire, or, perhaps, as the spirits did — with the stone axes to be found today when the present occupants of This Layer make their new gardens.

Möawä and his people desperately wanted a reliable source of good machetes. For this they were willing to set aside past grievances: including the death of a father, his skull crushed by an ax.

Like all Yąnomamö groups, even the strongest, Möawä's needed friends. But no one can openly admit a need for allies. This implies weakness, and weakness invites predation. To foster an alliance, the Yąnomamö deal in trade items — pots, baskets, dogs — and rely on them to create bonds between giver and recipient.

This proceeds as though the item itself is charged with a mystical quantity that puts the recipient under an inescapable obligation to repay the first gift with another. Thus both parties become less likely to be hostile.

As FRIENDSHIP grows, trade goods remain its theme. Indeed, one group may stop producing things it needs — just to get them from another. With such "specialized production" go claims like this: "Oh, we don't know how to raise cotton. We get that from the Mömariböwei-teri." When these neighbors turn hostile, people promptly "remember" how to raise cotton, or make baskets, or whatever.

So, in political dealings, these proud men do not imperil their dignity. The alliance, in their eyes, was born of a need for material possessions and nothing more. When it grows cold, and all alliances eventually do, the transient peace changes imperceptibly toward war.

No alliance outweighs independence among the Yąnomamö. Each group must remain free to pursue its own destiny. The tribal village, like the nation state, is jealous of its freedom to act as it wills, for its own ends. Peace with honor becomes more a pursuit of policy than of peace.

In this kind of politics, exchanges of decorative feathers or curare-smeared arrowheads take on the aura of negotiations over crown jewels. Rightly so, for these are delicate moments for all. Status, not wealth, is involved. And when a machete changes hands, it pronounces the relative importance of giver and recipient.

Thus Kąobawä's group and Möawä's met as sovereign equals, and this made the situation even touchier. Eventually one group would emerge as superordinate, but no one would hint at such a thing now. Initial negotiations are exquisitely polite.

To create the most sociable context, men choose suitable kinship terms. The most prominent call each other "shoriwä," brother-in-law, to indicate their friendship.

"Shoriwä! I am happy to see you after such a long time! I notice that your people still make the best arrows I have ever seen! That one lying there, next to you, is especially beautiful — and my dearest brother, that lad there, is without good arrows!

Notice that he carries an ugly, worn-out machete on his waist string.

"Would you possibly consent to give your magnificent arrow to that unfortunate lad in return for his worthless, scruffy machete?" The arrow is badly damaged from hunting. The machete is new.

"Aaaahh! Shoriwä! Yes! Yes! I will give this worthless arrow to your dear brother, but my arrow is so poor, so unworthy a gift for such a valuable machete! Let me throw in that mangy dog over there, the one that belongs to my son-in-law. Perhaps someday we might visit your village, and you could give my son-in-law a hammock for his dog." The dog is, in fact, mangy.

The son-in-law blushes, puts his arrows down, finds a vine, ties the dog's legs together, and carries him over to the new owner: "*Bei!* — Take him as yours!"

Presently items are passing back and forth, creating social ties that have no correlation with the merits of the things exchanged. Each group ends up with the other's possessions — dogs, arrows, bows. In a purely material sense, neither gained nor lost anything. But all the participants are now bound by promise, by the power of obligation to repay debts.

Such trade does not involve economic value as we measure it, and a century of untrained observers have retreated, scratching their collective heads, because a native system like this does not yield itself to our notions of scarcity and profit.

Only such exotic items as machetes, things made by foreigners, distort the established patterns of trade and alliance.

Kąobawä's men spent hours trading with their hosts. We all slept more easily that night. Artful speeches had guided the first steps toward a peace, and lavish promises of exchange forged scores of social links among former enemies. This is the indispensable stuff of politics: reciprocity and obligation, the giving of goods and the

Arrowpoints fell man and beast. Thin palmwood points dipped in curare bring down monkeys. Wider ones of bamboo find use in warfare; decorative markings identify the maker. The barb on the bird-point (far left) comes from a monkey's shinbone. Jaguar fur lines the quiver cap.

SHAMATARI QUIVER, ACTUAL LENGTH 14 3/4 INCHES; COURTESY NAPOLEON
A. CHAGNON; N.G.S. PHOTOGRAPHERS VICTOR R. BOSWELL, JR., AND ROBERT S. OAKES

promise of more, the creation of social indebtedness where none existed.

A new day carried friendship even further. The visitors had brought a supply of hallucinogen as a gift for Dedeheiwä, whose renown as a shaman they knew from afar.

In addition to possessing mortal truth, he was famed for his superb ability to speak with the myriad of ageless spirits—the hekura—who came into being when the cosmos was young and tender.

He ordered the drug prepared. Younger men carefully unwrapped the leaf-package of *hisiomö* seeds to knead them between their palms, adding saliva to moisten the pulp, ashes from *Ama* bark to make it less astringent. When it reached the proper consistency, they dried it on a heated sherd from a broken pot and ground it into a fine powder with one of the stone axes that the spirits left behind.

Using a length of cane called *mokohiro*, they began to blow this *ebene* powder into each other's nostrils. The hallucinogen enables them to invoke the hekura spirits, to summon them with magical incantations from their mountain homes. The hekura, beautiful themselves, are attracted by beauty—paint, feathers, fragrance, flawless and melodious songs—and shamans adorn themselves with paint or brilliant plumes.

B EFORE LONG, Dedeheiwä, streaked with red pigment and perspiration, was prancing back and forth before his house, chanting softly to the hekura, calling them from their hills to his breast.

Only by due abstinence and preparation may one become worthy to see the hekura; but in this rite I see an intense, dedicated man. For this is the only source of healing, and by it he cures his sick daughter, or another of his sixteen children, or the child of a sister. Here is a man who takes responsibility very seriously.

I see, in this activity, another dimension to Dedeheiwä's extraordinary virtuosity. Like Faust, he is accomplished at many things; but unlike Faust, he does not surrender himself to the spirits when he makes his pacts. He demands that the spirits surrender themselves to him. And when he calls to them, they come.

Often he has told me of these visions. First to arrive are the fragrant hekura, who anoint his body with attractive odors that no mortal shall ever be privileged to know. Next come the hot and meat-hungry hekura, prancing and reeling through the sky, resplendent with fiery halos and indescribably magnificent decorations, dancing wildly down their individual trails.

They enter his feet, traverse the inner trails of his body, and come to rest in the spiritual shabono he has within his chest. Each has prodigious abilities to travel through the sky to enemy villages and devour the souls of people there.

A week earlier they would have been sent against Kaobawä's people, now they are sent against others.

Dedeheiwä stops momentarily, squats near his son Yoaiyobowä, and commands him to offer more of the ebene. The young man picks up his father's mokohiro, pushes a small quantity of snuff into one end with his forefinger, carefully adjusts the placement of the long tube. He takes a deep breath and blows the enchanting powder forcefully into his father's nasal passages.

The old man shudders, winces, coughs uncontrollably and rises to his feet to continue his drama with the hekura, his vision and perception clearer now. He sends his spirits to consume souls in hostile villages; the victims sicken and die. He exorcises the agents of sickness from his own village, keeping his people free from incursions of hekura sent by enemies.

He sings about the mythical world, about Giant Toucan, the first hekura, and how he came into being. This was accomplished when the ancestors, who were part human and part spirit, destroyed Opossum—for Opossum, out of jealousy, had treacherously killed his brother the Beautiful One with harmful magic. Also he sings of Jaguar and the origin of vengeance.

His kinsmen watch and listen, and learn about the spirits and creation from the man who speaks with those that created.

For this is an ordered universe of kinship, linking mortal men and women to one another—and to the spirits who themselves were, in the past, more human.

While this strong order survives, not even I, the supposedly dispassionate observer, can evade its patterns. Following Yanomamö custom, I avoid those women who call me "son-in-law." I can joke with those I call "cross-cousin," the women who would be my marriage partners.

For reasons I still do not understand, Dedeheiwä decided that he and I are "brothers-in-law." This usage places me in his generation and, incidentally, raises my status; perhaps it was his way of looking out for me. As brothers-in-law we can be intimate friends; we can joke about sex, even at each other's expense. Ideally, I would marry his sisters and he would marry mine; our children could marry each other.

Others would be more aloof—men I call "father" and those I call "brother."

Möawä addresses me as *aba:* elder brother. "Aba" usually implies a measure of affection, but that warmth easily yields to tone of voice or subtle gestures that emphasize formality.

Within the cooler range implied by "aba," Möawä and I undertook to behave in an acceptable way—for kinship terms carry prescriptions of behavior. We both knew from the outset that we would be sizing each other up, for we are too much alike to make either of us comfortable.

I believe it was very difficult for him to gauge how fully I had become "human" by his culture's definitions or how clearly I knew the subtleties of Yąnomamö brotherhood—the nuances of command and compliance in his, the most perfect of all human societies.

Möawä makes inexorable demands, and his brothers know they must obey or they must leave. We both knew it would be wise to avoid a test of wills. Therefore I sometimes pretended not to understand his "wishes"—a form of slyness that smacked of insubordination, something he would not ignore but could not act upon openly. The myth of Opossum's fratricidal jealousy seemed to pervade our relationship... myths are not remote fairy tales to the Yąnomamö. They live within their past, among their spirits.

Ohina *cuttings will yield starchy roots—a minor staple. Men slash and burn an area, plant crops among the felled timbers, do minimal weeding.*

Listening to Dedeheiwä chant the stories of the mythical world, or discussing it with Kạobawä, I recognize that Jaguar—Öra—generates a tremendous awe, almost a reverence, among their people. They are not unique in this. Jaguar inspired the Chavín culture of Peru three thousand years ago, and continues to inspire other South American tribes.

To the Yạnomamö, Jaguar represents, like man himself, a predator of extreme competence in the hunt. Like man, he also hunts men. To say that he hunts other men would not be inappropriate, for there is, in the eyes of the Yạnomamö, something hauntingly sapient about Jaguar.

HE IS a creature of the Feral world that cannot be tamed, but he possesses a cunning peculiarly human. He is part human, part animal, part spirit. He straddles the chasm that separates the domain of Nature from the domain of Culture.

As lords of their own realm, the Yạnomamö know that their arrows and, more important, their fires give them an undeniable advantage over Jaguar. Yet his occasional human kills remind men that their dominance is fragile.

More than once I have been awakened by the pleas of my friends: "My father left this morning on a visit and didn't make it home! He is alone! He is in the jungle with no fire! Jaguars will surely kill and eat him! Bring your gun and flashlight and help us find him before it is too late!"

Off we would go, in the pitch black of night, into the jungle to find a kinsman . . . who would weep in gratitude when we arrived before Jaguar.

In myth, Jaguar emerges as a vicious, clumsy, cannibalistic brute, bent on destroying humanity but always falling short of his goal because men outwit him.

One Yạnomamö myth, with elements widespread in South America, recounts his insatiable demand for human flesh. Only a few survivors remain, including his "mother-in-law," Mamokoriyoma—Curare. As her name implies, she is bitter and Jaguar will not eat her. She hides her pregnant daughter in the leaves of the shabono roof, directly over Jaguar's hammock. He discovers her, kills her, and begins to devour her before her mother's eyes.

The old woman asks for the fetus as her share in the meal, and Jaguar tosses it to her. She puts it into a container of water,

where it is transformed into twin heroes: Omawä and Yoawä. They grow miraculously into adults and flee from the village, with Jaguar in pursuit.

A long sequence of near-captures follows, but in each case the Twins make a fool of him. They trick him into situations that end in debasing embarrassments, and Jaguar's stupidity leads him to fall into thorn patches, fall out of trees, and become the butt of a host of insults.

One tells such stories smugly in the comfort of a bustling shabono, around the flickering campfires. It is a different matter in the jungle, the terrain that Jaguar claims as beyond dispute his own.

Once I was traveling to Dedeheiwä's village with two companions. The first night we camped, they roused me several times to borrow my only flashlight: "Pssst! Shaki! Wake up! I have to urinate and I'm afraid to walk out there in the dark—I might step on a snake, or run into a jaguar! Lend me your *huu* so I can see where I'm going!"

At our second camp I gave them my light before we retired. About four in the morning I woke with my companions shouting hysterically into my ear: "*Öra! Öra! Öra!*" By the time I got unscrambled from my blanket, I caught only a glimpse of Jaguar's shadow, eerie in the moonlight, disappearing silently into the black jungle a few yards to my right. Our fire had gone out, and he was hunting. A low voice hissed into my ear: "When I heard his cry I flashed the light on him! He was ready to pounce on *you!* I was terrified!"

A few years later, not many miles from that very spot, I was standing on a desolate sandbar in the river, taking star shots with a theodolite for map-making. It was a coal-black, quiet evening. My single companion was sleeping comfortably, a wad of fresh chewing tobacco in his lip. I was lost in my work, oblivious to the jungle twenty yards away at my back.

A low cough, followed by an almost infantlike whine, reminded me that I was in Jaguar's domain. I hastily returned to my companion, stoked up the fire until it roared, and told him we might have company. A society of two people is a very small one, but I felt more comfortable, confident that even this social unit could overcome nature. One was insufficient, and without fire even two were not enough.

Jaguar, as he straddles the gap between

Culture and Nature, appears to pull them inexorably together. Only fire can keep the necessary gap there, for if the embers die and grow cold, men pass with alarming ease from one domain to the other. They admit it only by denying it in myth.

The Yąnomamö seem to fear that they will turn into cannibalistic were-jaguars, a theme that runs through a number of myths, a theme that they find repugnant and despicable. Whenever I killed a tapir and fried steaks—rare and bloody—and ate them in front of my comrades, they were revolted. They could not bear to watch me eat "raw" flesh.

"You want to turn into a jaguar! You want to eat people! We will never give you any meat if you behave that way! Only jaguars eat that way!" They had patiently made their subhuman visitor near-human by teaching it language, and it could yet be so Feral. They found this contrast most disgusting.

Age contrasts with youth. Dedeheiwä once stalked now-abandoned trails to exact vengeance with bamboo-tipped arrows. Now his son-in-law Möawä haunts these mortal trails, while the aging Dedeheiwä concerns himself with the spiritual paths that link him to his beloved hekura, and he teaches his sons about them.

I have learned other contrasts of this world . . . the incessant brilliance of the Equatorial sun in January alternates with the colorless skies of May and the constant rains that come with them; and the quiet, shadowy pools of crystal water differ from the mud-choked torrents that call them into being, filling them in the wet months, abandoning them in the dry.

The happy chatter of children, delicately and gently grooming each other, contrasts with the severity of the adult world, where the men they will replace duel with their fists, with clubs—or take up their bows and lie in wait, in the shadow of some distant shabono, waiting for an enemy to step outside, unsuspecting, and fall under a volley of arrows . . . and call for his mother, who cannot help him then.

And this contrasts with peace, those uncertain periods when the snap of a twig after dark does not precipitate panic, those long exciting trips to distant villages to eat until your belly aches, to chant the new song you invented, and dance proudly before the admiring eyes of your joyous hosts.

With the other prominent men of their

village, Dedeheiwä and Möawä discussed Kąobawä's invitation to come and feast with him. They decided to accept it—but to leave their women and children at the mouth of the Washäwä River so as not to tempt the Bisaasi-teri men into foul play. New allies are uncertain friends, and it is best to proceed cautiously. A number of men would remain at home, because they had killed Bisaasi-teri and for them the risks were too great.

It would be a long journey—three weeks—for women and children cannot travel as swiftly as their unencumbered men. The leaders ordered young men to cut large quantities of plantains and cache them along the line of march. Large groups cannot rely on the jungle to provide vegetable foods.

Such trips are like vacations to the Yąnomamö, for they can forget about gardening or chopping endless logs into firewood. A day away from the village, game is always plentiful; and the forest supplies materials for three-cornered huts, huts that soon decay and leave no sign that 200 people passed along a trail.

AFTER MANY DAYS the Mishimishimaböwei-teri men reached Kąobawä's village. Their arrival sparked excitement among all, especially among a few old women who had not seen their kinsmen for many years—they had been abducted by Bisaasi-teri raiders when they were *moko,* tender and ripening, like a maturing banana.

Yanayanarima wept when she heard that Dedeheiwä was coming, her *abawä,* her dearest brother. They would relive the happy moments of their childhood, at a garden long since abandoned. She would weep when it came time for him to leave, for she could not go with him now. Her children and grandchildren were Bisaasi-teri, and she could not leave them.

The feast was like all feasts—boiled plantain soup and boiled peach-palm fruits; a mound of smoked monkeys, armadillos, tapir, and wild turkeys. Everywhere men exchanged promises of gift and counter-gift. The young flirted and strutted in their crimson paint and gaudy feathers, the leaders planned and plotted.

It was decided that the visitors would help Kąobawä raid the Patanowä-teri, for he had not yet avenged their killing of a brother. His surviving brothers tenderly brought out the victim's arrowpoint quiver, smashed it, and wept bitterly as the flames consumed it. They wept and moaned, Shamatari and Bisaasi-teri alike, as Torokoiwä carefully unpacked a last gourd of cremated bones, poured a little of the gray ash into a gourd of hot plantain soup, stirred it with his hands, and passed it to the dead man's sisters to drink.

A Shamatari took the log effigy his young allies had spent the afternoon making, and dragged it into the plaza. Kąobawä said it was his brother Rakoiwä: one of the headmen of the village to be raided, killer of his other brother. The Shamatari warrior approached the effigy and abused it with coarse insults, beat it with a club, and spat contemptuously on it.

Men put it into a hammock and Kąobawä ordered the raiders to attack it. They crept up to it slowly, and at his signal they rose, aimed, and sent a volley of bamboo-tipped arrows into the dense wood. "Rakoiwä" rattled to the ground.

Raiders leave—as they strike—at dawn. The morning dampness and cold had not yet been expelled from the village when the scream and growl of the first raider drew everyone's attention to the plaza. The dogs howled and a few babies began crying.

Covered with black paint, the growling raider paced slowly to the center of the clearing, clacking his arrows against his bow, and faced to the southeast, toward the enemy. He stood there silently. An oppressive gloom lay over the shabono.

A scream and a growl shattered it, and another dark figure walked slowly out and stood beside the first, trembling with anxiety. Another followed from a different quarter, then another—until the silent line stretched from one end of the village to the other, expressionless and sinister.

Kąobawä emerged and called them around him. They shouted in high-pitched screams, and rattled their arrows ecstatically when they heard the sound return. It came from Patanowä-teri: the *no uhudibö*—echo and soul—of their victims.

The warriors marched out, single file, and did not look back. Their women sobbed and turned their faces away as they disappeared into the garden, into the jungle. I switched my tape recorder off and began packing my cameras. I recalled with a twinge of anger that the Patanowä-teri had recently raided Kąobawä, and that they had made several log effigies . . . men they wanted to kill. One of them was of me.

My enemy's friend is my enemy....

My freedom to move among these hostile groups was becoming very restricted now, and I had become too much a part of what I had come to observe.

The attack on Patanowä-teri would be on the third dawn. The days passed. I was interviewing an old woman in my mud-and-thatch hut when I heard excited shouts. Dashing to the village, I saw Kąobawä sag wearily into his hammock; I went to him.

"*Shoabe!* Did all return?" He raised his eyebrows: all had returned.

"Did you reach Patanowä-teri?"

"No. I turned back, and when I did, the others gave up and followed me."

Startled, I asked why.

"I slept two nights. On the third I had a dream. In my dream Jaguar devoured me, and I knew that I would be killed if I continued." Privately I was happy that Jaguar's domain was not confined to darkness and Nature and that my father-in-law was safe, safe at home.

ONCE it had troubled me that Kąobawä could be so vindictive toward a brother. That was when my leaves possessed more wisdom than my soul did, when I first lived among the Yąnomamö. After this abortive raid I made repeated visits to Mishimishimaböwei-teri, and my relationship with my younger brother Möawä deteriorated by a law of its own being. We came closer and closer to the incident we both foresaw.

In 1972, when I returned to his village, he greeted me without the courtesies of custom and set upon me with unnegotiable public demands, hissing surly orders between his teeth: "You are not to give any of your tidbits to the brats in this village—if anything is to be eaten, I will eat it.... You will give me all of your eye-medicine and not share it with the others.... You will give all of your trade goods to me immediately; you will not give others your machetes."

He had realized that if I knew the myths of his people, I simply had to understand ordinary Yąnomamö. I could not pretend to be ignorant; I could not obey him and still collect the information I needed from his kinsmen in the next village—the men he had driven out.

As luck would have it, they were visiting his group. Hastily I set about my work in spite of him, collecting data, paying with my machetes—paying important men with followers of their own, men who had defied Möawä before. Everyone knew a crisis was at hand. Many looked forward to it, and some would take my side. These were the visitors, Möawä's brothers.

One machete remained when he learned I had defied him. He burst through the crowd, ax in hand, and rushed at me shaking with anger. We saw each other in the simplest of human terms. I glared into his cold eyes and measured him as closely as he measured me. His knuckles grew whiter as he clutched the ax, poised over my head.

Despite his passion, he gradually lowered the ax, hissing a final order: "This machete belongs to that man over there! Don't you dare give it to these thieves around you. They are not my villagers."

I "gave" the man the machete as Möawä ordered, and he did not threaten me again before I left, the next day. I do not like to think that I shall never see Dedeheiwä again, but I do not expect to return to my brother's village while my brother lives.

I understand why my father-in-law, a measured and fair man, can lead raiders against his brothers. I understand why Möawä and Kąobawä will inevitably quarrel. They are made of the same stuff, but in different combinations.

They lead political groups of the kind that lie but dimly in our own past, contemporary expressions of a dimension that seems foreign to us now. They are still among us, condemned to a fleeting twilight in a time that shall never again be known to men, a generation removed that I had the privilege of joining to make my imperfect and inadequate observations ... to journey through an intimate and inner space which cannot be represented in the genealogies that are its most certain trails.

I understand fully where I have been, what I did when I walked there. I am convinced that the Kąobawäs in our lineage were the indispensable links that have led to our success—but, ironically, only because there were also Möawäs. They are in truth, as my teacher Elman Service has reminded us, our contemporary ancestors.

Chanting, rapt in a shaman's visions, Möawä welcomes ageless and lovely spirits called hekura *to his breast.*

After two decades of war, enemies meet—as diplomats. Leaning forward earnestly, visiting headman Kąobawä of Bisaasi-teri tells leaders of Mishimishimaböwei-teri that blame for the hostilities indeed rests with a

third village. Through lengthy orations charged with tension and ostentatious good will, the men agree on an acceptable version of history. They minimize once-important grievances, and open the way to an alliance of mutual benefit.

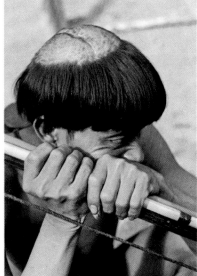

Proud of his scars from duels with clubs, a warrior keeps his skull shaven to reveal them — a hairstyle also prized for its own sake. Men display their fierceness in a variety of ways, but all take part in ceremonies. Visitors (overleaf) dance in anticipation of a feast. They enter the village two by two and circle in opposite directions, strutting and parading for the admiring throng. Then all gather in the center of the village, waving their weapons over-head and shouting, while the hosts noisily praise their beauty and ferocity.

In varied proofs of force, the waiteri, fierce ones, enact—and limit—aggression. Chest-pounding duels permit blows with clenched fist; a good fighter will take as many as four before claiming his right to return them. A more violent ritual allows an exchange of wallops on the head with heavy but limber clubs. At Kąobawä's village, as a conclusion to mortuary rites after enemy raiders killed his brother, young men wrestle to express sorrow and anger; brandished axes and clubs indicate that hostility may flare out of control—always a danger in any Yąnomamö contest. But a duel may also demonstrate friendship at the end of a feast, an occasion when men's duties include the ceremonial cooking of rasha palm fruit (overleaf).

With a blast of air through a length of cane, headman Möawä blows a dose of hallucinogen deep into the nasal passages of Yarabiawä, a young fellow villager. Yarabiawä will react at once and violently: Coughing and retching, he will rise and reel about the compound, mucus streaming from his irritated nose. Then, in a state of trance, he will welcome the hekura, spirits capable of destroying the souls of enemies in distant villages. Beauty attracts the hekura, so he adorns himself with paint and feathers and chants enticing melodies. At left, a man prepares one of the drugs for use—all of them potent, none of them habit-forming. After drying the leaves of a cultivated shrub on a potsherd over a fire, he combines them with ashes from bark and pulverizes the mixture into a finely powdered snuff.

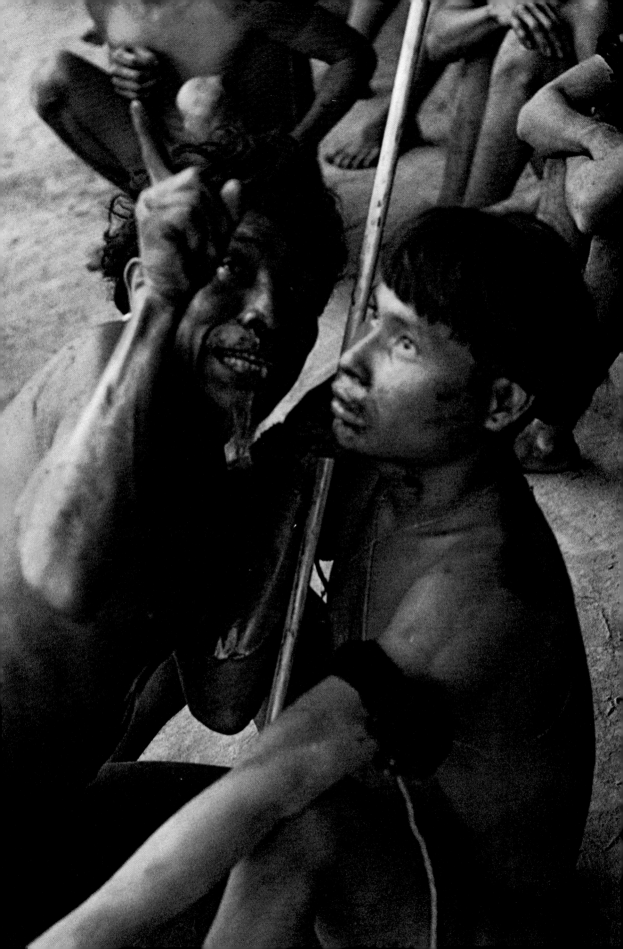

Dedeheiwä, respected far beyond his own village, evokes a mystery to share with a young son as he instructs him in the art of shamanism, his own unending study. The Yąnomamö attribute all sickness to harmful magic or to hekura sent from the enemy; to effect a cure the shaman must exorcise the invisible agent or extract it forcibly from its victim's body. With great, impassioned exertion a healer struggles—and succeeds. Death from battle wounds lies beyond supernatural aid, but shamans spare no effort against illness, and often, triumphantly, they see their patients recover.

Circular shabono of this Yąnomamö village houses some 125 people. A shabono lasts only a year or two; when the overlapping palm leaves of the roof dry out and become infested with insects, the residents burn the structure and build another. Men construct new individual homes in a big circle, about three feet apart, then roof over the gaps—a month's work in itself. Cramped entryways lead to surrounding gardens of plantains and manioc. At left, turquoise waters of the Orinoco River reflect distant Mount Duida. In 1800 the great German explorer and naturalist Baron von Humboldt, seeking the source of the Orinoco, reached this area and found a small party of Yąnomamö—their first encounter with a scientist. Rather than risk trouble with such formidable warriors, he turned back downriver.

Tug-of-war in the rain pits women and children of Mishimishimaböwei-teri against one another; a few older boys even the odds when one side appears to be winning. Young men frolic in the afternoon at the swimming hole, deepest

part of the stream that provides the water supply. A trail to the village crosses the creek on the log. "It's quite slippery," says the author. "I used to fall off logs like this at first and everybody found it funny—even me."

Her pack-basket crammed with 50 pounds of firewood, a woman heads homeward. Women spend several hours daily gathering wood, often searching several miles for it. In times of war this exposes them to raiders, and men sometimes join them for protection —but not to help carry the load. At left, Kąobawä's niece weaves a hammock from cotton the Yąnomamö cultivate and spin. Decorative sticks protrude from her pierced lower lip. Between such active games as shooting tiny arrows at crickets in the roof, youngsters groom one another, carefully and gently.

Warrior of a Shamatari village aims a cane arrow 6$\frac{1}{2}$ feet long. The bow, carved from palmwood with the canine teeth of a wild pig, can drive an arrow through a tapir's hide—or two inches deep into a hardwood log. Preparing hunting arrows, which his village trades to allies, Dedeheiwä steadies a bundle while his brother paints a tip with curare, poison from the bark of a vine. As they apply coat after coat, the fire evaporates excess liquid. Below, a traveler pauses for a drink. He collected his plantain cuttings at an abandoned garden; his knife arrived with trade goods introduced in recent years.

Exuberant and well-fed guests parade around Ką̃obawä's village with a bark trough they have just emptied of banana soup and will soon toss into the bushes. Protocol demands the loud display as well as the finery. A little girl painstakingly fashions an apron of flowers; boys climb a towering forest tree for these blooms—but only to give them to girls. Both men and women enjoy beautifying themselves with blossoms, paint in varied patterns, and feathers. A pet white-throated toucan, a bird prominent in Yą̃nomamö myth, perches on the arm of its fond young owner.

Pre-raiding rituals: Allied warriors of Mishimishimaböwei-teri and Bisaasi-teri drink banana soup—and strengthen the bonds soon to be proved in a raid on a mutual foe. At right, men attack an effigy of one of the enemy: Kąobawä's brother. Led by Kąobawä, they place a painted log in a hammock, stalk it, and shoot it full of arrows. At dawn, the raiders—each with his weapons ready—line up behind Dedeheiwä's son for a final exhortation. But on this occasion, after two nights on the trail, Kąobawä dreamed a jaguar was devouring him; he turned back at this omen, and his party returned with him.

*Chanting diplomats exchange vows of
friendship as a visit between their
two villages nears an end. Setting
aside old grievances, men may chant
all morning, promising to trade
valued goods — not for profit but
for social considerations. One may even
barter a new machete for a worthless
arrow, for instance, thus imposing an
almost sacred obligation on the recipient.
"If you measure political character
by effort," says the author, "the
Yąnomamö are far more 'peacelike'
than warlike, for they devote much
more effort to creating and maintaining their fragile alliances
of peace." Chest-pounding duels and
fights with clubs relieve passions that
might otherwise lead to battle;
shared rituals and softened versions
of the truth help old enemies
forget the bloody past.*

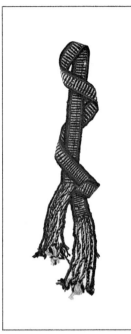

7

TARAHUMARA

Crosses of the four winds,
corn of summer gold

by Tor Eigeland
Photographs by the author

JUST EAST of the center of a clearing in thorn scrub and cactus stood a crude altar topped by three wooden crosses, all draped in white muslin. Six feet to its left, another cloth-covered wooden cross was driven into the ground.

When Melecio and I stumbled onto this *patio* after hours on the steep trails of Batopilas Canyon, men in white breechcloths and white shirts with puffed sleeves were preparing for some kind of ceremony. Women watched, vivid figures in multiple layers of colorful skirts, red blouses, white headbands three inches wide. Unwilling to intrude, we quickly greeted the people and found a seat on a slope about 50 yards away—evidently a polite distance, for no one gave any sign of objections.

Harsh noon sunlight and crystal air let us see the proceedings clearly when a bareheaded old man tried to wrestle a cow to the ground. Three youths with white-and-red headbands ran to help him. Two old

In the high canyon country of northern
Mexico a goatherd watches as his flock
finds spring browse on a distant hillside.

women stood by and giggled until the cow was down. The men tied its legs together and lashed it to a stake behind the neck. The boys pulling away on the tail and the old man tugging away at the head, they turned the animal so its exposed throat faced east toward the altar, then west, north, south, back to the east again.

One of the women handed the old man a gourd-shaped pot of *morewaka*, smoking incense. He walked behind the cow, waved the container three times toward the altar, three times away from it, three times to the north, to the south, then made a line of smoke above the animal. He repeated this at the altar.

During a brief trip to this forbidding Mexican mountain country ten years earlier I had seen very little, but enough to become fascinated with the mixture of aboriginal and 17th-century Spanish customs that the Tarahumara Indians have preserved here. I knew that now by a great stroke of luck we were witnessing a rite of just this character.

Possibly the crosses themselves still symbolized the four cardinal directions, revered in Mexico long before the white

PURACA, OR SASH; ACTUAL LENGTH 6 FEET; COURTESY TOR EIGELAND;
PHOTOGRAPH BY JOSEPH H. BAILEY, N.G.S. STAFF

man came, or the four winds. An old Indian had once told me that when they use three crosses, one is for the Sun, God of the Men, the second is for the Moon, God of the Women, and the third for the Morning Star.

A knife was stuck in the wooden altar below us. The old man, host for the occasion and also a shaman, jerked it out and slit the jugular vein of the cow while the boys held it down. An old woman caught the blood in a wooden bowl and handed a small spoon to the shaman. He dipped it into the bowl and, standing up, tossed blood three times toward the altar, in the other three directions, once straight up.

The same ritual was performed with a goat at the single cross. The old man killed six chickens less formally, twirling them around by the neck two at a time in front of the altar. An ancient woman carried the blood away to be cooked while the men got busy butchering the animals.

My guide Melecio, a young Spanish-speaking Tarahumara from this region, said people would be busy preparing food for hours, and we climbed some 300 yards above the clearing to set up camp. As we worked, he told me: "The wife of the host went away a year ago. This is the last fiesta to help speed her on her way to heaven. When a man dies we have three fiestas. For a woman we have four since women are not as strong. If we do not help people go away they come back to bother our families—sometimes as animals."

The dramatic view from our campsite gave its own clues to the survival of rites like this. Canyon walls dropped a thousand feet below us, rose nearly vertical another two thousand feet higher—and gorges equally ragged extend mile after tortuous mile among the mountains of Chihuahua State. Even today, few outsiders make their way on foot or muleback very far into this country. Here and there a slope relieved the steep gray rock; where spurs of rock offered fairly level ground, scattered fields awaited cultivation.

Below us, quite far apart, were dwellings —stone houses with wooden or thatch roofs, caves with stone walls around the entrances—each with a corral for goats.

From a grove shaped like a cross, conspicuous in the thorny monotony below us, eddies of wind brought us whiffs of orange blossoms, though snow still lay in patches high on the cliff. A few buzzards cruised

In twisting gorges with few roads, on mountainsides with many rock-strewn trails, some 50,000 Tarahumaras retain customs brought from 17th-century Spain—and the ways of their forebears, older still.

in the cobalt sky, invisible birds were chirping, distant drums bounced their sounds back and forth between the canyon walls. Vaguely, we could hear the Batopilas River rumbling among the boulders far below — and then something stranger: faint, mumbled, eerie.

"They are about to start the *tutuguri*," said Melecio. A man draped in a blanket was moving slowly back and forth in front of the altar, shaking a rattle and chanting. "He is the *sawéame* — the man who plays the maraca — he will do this all night."

A file of eight women, holding hands, came out to the sawéame's right; when he turned to face them they started dancing — a simple shifting of the feet, a little hop. They repeated their dance on occasion during the night, while the sawéame continued his chant with only brief pauses.

The fiesta grew more lively as the guests, about forty in all, started to drink *tesgüino*, a corn beer. At one point *matachine* dancers, men with clothes and headdresses as glittering as Christmas trees, whirled swiftly around shaking rattles while the solemn tutuguri was still going on and a third group, men and women together, danced the slow *yúmari* to the notes of homemade violins and guitars. Coyote-like shouts and raucous laughter and mock war cries produced a human din that rose to the blackness of the mountains, the huge sky.

Morning sun found the Indians still dancing. Women brought food and set it on the altar; the shaman "cured" it with the incense ceremony and raised the brimful gourds three times in each direction.

"That's *tónari*," explained Melecio. "All night they boiled the cow, the goat, and the chickens with some corn, beans, and herbs." It was a great treat since the Tarahumaras seldom kill livestock except for sacrifice.

The tesgüino ran out about noon; the guests who had not already dropped off to sleep somewhere staggered home.

Not all the people around had been invited to the fiesta. Near our camp, with her back against a big rock, a woman was weaving a blanket on a loom with a square log frame, mounted horizontally on four rocks; and farther down the trail, outside his cave, a young man named Jesús Ramírez sat on a rock cutting the wooden frame for a goatskin drum, an instrument used only from February till Easter.

We exchanged greetings — "*Kwira-bá*" — and I sat down on a rock to watch the work.

Jesús had typical Tarahumara looks: black hair in a type of pageboy cut, brown skin, high cheekbones, a slightly flat nose and a wide mouth; fine bone structure and muscular, slender arms and legs. Like everyone in the sierra, he wore sandals made from old tires, with thin leather straps. It occurred to me that I had never seen a fat Tarahumara man, or a bald one.

I broke the silence that bothers no one in Tarahumara land, and made small talk — an indication that I had something important to say eventually: "That's going to be a fine drum." "Drum, drum," mumbled Jesús in Spanish. After leisurely general conversation I got to the point: "I hear that you are making tesgüino. Could you show me how?" Jesús got up and gestured for me to follow him into the cave.

Probably its ceiling had accumulated layers of soot for centuries, and the back wall seemed almost as dark, but when Jesús removed a covering of damp green leaves I could recognize sprouting grains of corn. "It takes five days or so for the corn to sprout," said Jesús. "Today my wife will grind it on a metate, then we boil it with water." "How do you make it ferment?" I asked. (I knew the time required varies with the weather.) "We grind *basiáwi* — brome grass — and add it after the boiling. Tomorrow we will drink tesgüino."

Tesgüino is more important to the Tarahumara than beer to the Australian. The shaman uses it when blessing people, animals, fields, or the harvest. When someone needs a big job done, like weeding a field, he invites friends to drink tesgüino; they do the work and receive tesgüino in return.

Reserved in manner — at least with outsiders — Tarahumara families live scattered in difficult country; and individuals are often alone working remote plots of ground or herding goats. When people gather in groups tesgüino serves as a release; they become animated, often rowdy. Fighting and adultery, the most serious sources of trouble, take place almost exclusively at drinking sessions. People drink to get drunk, and frankly say so.

"Why do you drink tomorrow?" I asked Jesús. "We are going to be cured," he said. Curing sometimes acts as a preventive measure, at other times as an actual healing of disease, and Jesús meant the former.

Rituals, Roman Catholic and aboriginal, started to get mixed up more than 300 years ago, when the first Jesuit missionaries arrived, and something distinctively Tara-humara emerged. The great majority of the Tarahumaras have been baptized and when a priest comes they attend his services. Otherwise, they have their own.

When Melecio and I reached Jesús' cave next morning, the shaman was already there, with the *gobernador*, "governor," a local official. They were curing the home and the hosts of the party with incense and smoking corncobs. Jesús' little boy got his hair singed by a cob and screamed in terror, much to everyone's amusement. People arrived in their most colorful clothes, and finally the shaman blessed the tesgüino itself. With a small dipper he tossed some of the liquid three times in each of the four directions, once straight up.

Now the drinking could commence. To my surprise, the shaman held out the communal gourd first to me. Perhaps I held it wrong or looked uneasy, for there was a subdued, polite laughter from the crowd. I found tesgüino pleasant, with the taste of beer and the consistency of a milkshake.

As the drinking hit its stride we left, casually, without anyone paying attention. It is good to be able to leave a party that way; and good to make camp alone after a day on incredibly steep trails. That evening we reached the settlement of Huimai-bo, in a valley at so low an elevation that it was warm even after dark—two miles from our starting point for a bird, nine hours' walk for us, an hour's trip for a local man.

Melecio was still asleep when, early next morning, I went to perch on a rock with a view of houses and cave-mouths. It was at least nine o'clock when smoke began to seep out between crudely cut boards. A man appeared on a flat wooden housetop, and I recognized the gobernador from yesterday. His wife came out of the house and sat down on a rock to apply a brush made from a pinecone to her long jet-black hair. The goats in the corral started to stir.

"Melecio! Listen. . . ." A hand reached out from under the blankets and groped for a Mexican sombrero. "The governor down there—what does he govern?"

"He makes justice for the Tarahumaras of Quirare, an area of a few square miles

Delighted to rejoin her family, Felicitas Guanapani (right) visits her home with a cousin and classmate, Lucía Nava. The author has helped sponsor her education.

around here. The men elect him and keep him until they are tired of him." "Is this a good governor?" "Yes, very good. Very strict. When my friend Laurencio got very drunk and started fighting at a tesgüino party the governor had his assistants hang him from a tree by the hands. Laurencio has behaved himself for a long time now."

Big and blazing, the sun leaped over the mountain crest about 10:30. Women and youngsters moved off into the scrub with the goats; men headed for the fields. I started down the arroyo with Melecio and when I waved to a man plowing a field he stopped, to my surprise, and waved back. He finished his last furrows, unhitched his two oxen, and only then came over to us.

This was Lupe Nava, "untypical" enough to talk a lot, and quite directly, in good Spanish. "The plots here are so small that I can do all my plowing in two days," he told me. "Do you have plots in the high sierra too?" "No, I am a poor man." For something to say, I looked at the plow: "Did the Tarahumaras always have a plow?" Lupe, as it turned out, had been to a Jesuit school and knew the right answer: "No, the Spanish brought the cattle and the plow 300 years ago. Before, we used the digging stick only, for we have always had corn. But look: progress"—a steel plowshare.

Lupe now did something no other Tarahumara had done. He made a suggestion related to what he realized was my work, and invited me to watch his wife make *pinole*—a corn beverage. This, with another called *esquiate*, is a staple of diet here.

Rosita Nava had just started shelling the corn, rubbing the cobs together, and Lupe joined in. She put some sand, then corn, into a clay jar and set it on the glowing embers of a fire. Lupe told me the sand helps distribute heat more evenly. As the kernels snapped, exactly like popcorn, she poured them into a loosely woven basket to shake out the sand. When all the corn was sifted, she got on her knees by the metate, a flat rock with a slight depression, and started grinding the kernels with a round stone. This she did three times.

That process took more than two hours, but mixing pinole is simplicity itself—pouring water into a gourd, adding the corn powder, and stirring. Pinole tastes slightly malty; I find it refreshing.

Lupe asked me straightforwardly if I had corn or goats or cows, and I had to say no. "Do you think I am poor?" I asked him.

"No—you probably have *lana*." *Lana* is a Mexican slang term for money. I had some questions of my own about livestock: "How do they make you rich when you do not milk them?" "Oh, we sometimes milk them to make cheese; and when we have fiestas we have them to sacrifice. And they make the corn grow." He explained how corrals are moved around the fields to fertilize them.

Lupe's home, a one-room structure with stone walls and a board roof, had all the necessities of life: three metates, big and small gourds, some large jars for tesgüino; wooden and metal spoons stuck in the wall; cloth bundles, bunches of herbs, and a banana stalk hanging from the ceiling; two blankets on some boards on the floor. Firewood was stacked against the wall, and soot covered the ceiling—the Tarahumaras never build chimneys, but let smoke escape as it will to the winds.

All the four winds seemed to blow at once, the day Melecio and I hiked out of Huimaibo. We could hear the whooshing sound of a gale whipping above us. Blasts of air whistled through the thorny brush at our level. A downpour struck as we reached the tiny mining town of La Bufa. All night, as cloudburst and gale continued, I could consider why one might sacrifice to these forces. Released by torrents of water, huge boulders crashed down the canyon walls, creating a frightening thunder that boomed back and forth.

The winds were still blowing, and bitter cold, when I reached the town of Creel in the highlands. However, warm friends welcomed me there. During my first trip to the sierra I had met Father Luis G. Verplancken, a young Jesuit missionary, and he and I had visited the settlement of Ojachichi, where we met an exceptionally smart and shy little Tarahumara girl: Felicitas Guanapani, age nearly 7.

At that time a cold wave ruled the sierra, people were hungry, and then as now innumerable children died before the age of 5, mostly of lung disease and malnutrition. Felicitas was by no means dying; but we brought her to a Jesuit boarding school, and I had helped sponsor her studies.

Felicitas, now 17, still smart, still shy, had spent one year at school in Louisiana and another in Colorado, with her inseparable friend and cousin Lucía Nava. They were eagerly awaiting me: I had promised to take them to Ojachichi.

The high country is bleak in winter. We drove on difficult logging trails through oak and pine forest. We had to walk the last cold two hours, loaded down with food and clothes and camera equipment, but nothing could dampen Felicitas' excitement. At a very effective short-stepped trot, the girls kept picking up speed.

At Ojachichi, families live scattered about beyond the little schoolhouse, small church, and shack for visiting priests—where I was to stay. Felicitas stood gazing down toward the arroyo: "My mother is there with her goats." I knew the great affection of this family, but the greeting was quiet—they slowly walked toward each other, brushed extended palms together, exchanged a few words, went separately to their log cabin. I never saw them more demonstrative than this.

Yet Felicitas' father, Juan, an affable, intelligent man about 45, was willing to talk with a minimum of reserve—a rare thing in this country. He told me how the *owirúame*, or shaman, cures people of sickness: dipping a crucifix in tesgüino and holding it in front of the body, holding a lighted candle before the body and turning to the four directions, maybe sucking "a worm" from the patient's chest. "Has he done this to you?" I asked. "Many times." "Did it help you?" "Yes, sometimes."

He took me to see rock paintings in red ocher: a life-size man with hands like chicken feet, holding something that might have been a deity; a stylized human riding something like a huge bug. "When were these done?" I asked. "They are from before"—an unvarying answer.

A friend of Juan's joined us to lead us to a site with a life-size hand, but would not approach it. Said Juan: "He tells me that many times at night things come out of there—like monkeys or people."

Like apparitions themselves, Tarahumara superstitions are not easily described. Melecio once opened a cave where his sister had been buried a year earlier. "What can we do to them?" he said to me. "They are already dead."

As we walked back, Juan pointed out the tracks of a puma in a patch of sand, and

Pots of tesgüino, *beer made from sprouted corn, will simmer, then ferment—to play a central role in ritual and social life.*

told me that wolves and bears were not far away. Some young men had killed five deer a few days earlier, running the animals down with their dogs and finishing them off with knives when they collapsed from exhaustion. "The Tarahumaras can run more than a deer," Juan added proudly.

Their name, in fact, is a Spanish corruption of *rarámuri*, "foot-runners." A young man can run 170 miles with only the briefest of stops, and their famous kick-ball races provide a good deal of excitement.

I saw a local race at Ojachichi—two teams of three men each, and two wooden balls about the size of a baseball—but I would never have noticed the trickiest part if Juan hadn't pointed it out. When the racer comes up to the ball he stops for an almost imperceptible fraction of a second and gives it a lift-kick off the top of his toes. This race covered about 30 miles along the river, in less than four hours. During the last lap young girls ran cheering alongside their men, but when the winner had kicked the ball across the finish line he just sat down alone on a rock. Never did I see the Indians make a fuss over a winner.

And when I left with Lucía and Felicitas, neither Juan nor his wife came out to say goodbye. On the way to Creel, however, Felicitas said something that touched me: "My father said he and his friends would fix the trail to Ojachichi so that next time you can drive all the way."

Back in Creel, she said, "Oh, it is terrible to be back in the town again!" She and Lucia dashed off for a hot bath—the one thing she really missed, she told me, whenever she went home.

At Creel I sought reasons why the Tarahumaras are still Tarahumaras in spite of disease, famine, wars, and an increasing contact with civilization.

My friend Father Verplancken, who speaks the language and has spent 21 of his 47 years in missionary work among the Tarahumaras, said: "They have kept their customs and rituals exactly the way they were 300 years ago. I have read letters written then, by the first missionaries; and my experiences with the Indian life match their descriptions exactly.

"Of course there are some changes in clothing now. And they want their children educated, to defend themselves against abuse by the whites. And some want trucks. But their rites and rituals, their way of thinking, are just the same."

Why? "Because they live in this inaccessible country, they never have intercommunal tribal meetings. Change does not spread beyond a few, and local traditions remain as they have for three centuries."

Robert Bye, an ethnobotanist who had spent a year in the sierra, commented: "Nobody really knows much about the Tarahumara culture because individuality appears to be the norm. People go their own way."

I asked Lucía Nava why there had been so little change: "Fear—fear of being robbed." Like many other Indians, the Tarahumaras have long been robbed and taken advantage of by whites and mestizos.

Both Lucía and Felicitas had ideas about what their people need, with the Chihuahua-Pacific Railroad bringing greater contact with the world outside. "They need to learn Spanish to be able to cope," said Lucía. "And to do some accounting," said Felicitas, "and learn about hygiene."

Father Verplancken and other missionaries are engaged in this sort of practical education. So is the Mexican government. Perhaps most helpful of all will be people like Felicitas and Lucía, who both plan to work among their own people.

FOR THREE CENTURIES, unchanged, the celebration of Easter has remained one of the year's biggest occasions among the Tarahumaras; and I chose the isolated settlement of Munérachi as a place to see the rituals in which some men destroy a straw dummy called "Judas" and others take on the roles of "Pharisees."

Undoubtedly most Tarahumaras would be hard put to explain any of this: Easter is a time for elaborate ceremony, the best clothes, a big party with lots of tesgüino.

On Thursday morning of Holy Week I arrived at the old adobe church of Munérachi, with Melecio. Many Indians were sitting about on nearby crags, others camped in the vicinity, a few already gathered at the church—but Melecio and I felt hostility so thick we were both a little scared.

Soon a man came up and told us we had to get out of there, on orders of the gobernador. It took hours of negotiation, as well as a gift of money for the celebration, before the gobernador sent word we could stay. Later we heard, with apologies, that because of a bad harvest the previous year government aid—corn—was supposed to have come. Like many promised things, the corn had not arrived; as outsiders, we were suspect in the matter.

Aside from three or four men with Mexican-style trousers and straw hats, the three hundred worshipers had proudly kept their traditional styles for new clothes in every color of cotton under the sun.

From the first, processions came and went. Pharisees with feather headdresses and long spears, and "soldiers" with wooden swords or wooden rifles, marched furiously in two circles in opposite directions around the gobernador. Every few hours they led him to the church for prayers in Tarahumara. There was no priest. One had been invited, but he had not been able to come.

Inside the church, left of the entrance, an old man played the flute continuously, joined at times by violins from the gallery upstairs. They all seemed to be playing different fragments of tunes, but the effect was an eerie harmony. The simplicity of furnishings enhanced this: only a bare wooden altar with a crucifix and a little statue of the Madonna, its paint faded.

From time to time two or three men would run around the church, outside, twirling wooden noisemakers that make a din like the chirring of giant grasshoppers. Men came and went playing drums in a simple boom-BOOM, boom-BOOM rhythm.

As dusk fell, more people gathered. Again the men with spears and the Pharisees went to fetch the gobernador. They marched double-quick around him and escorted him back into the church. As if on a signal hundreds of people swept into the church like a night-breeze. First the men, then the women.

With the gobernador and an old man officiating at the altar, prayers were said; then the crowd swished out again, now with lighted candles. Slowly they circled the church, stopping seven times during each round at two crosses placed side by side — Stations of the Cross. Whenever they halted, an old man led a rapid murmur of prayer and an even older woman, draped from head to toe in red cotton, held incense for blessing. Now the drums were silent. Beyond the prayers I heard only a single violin, a flute, gentle shuffling of feet. The air was heavy with incense and candles and the scent of flowering trees. "Christ would like this," I thought.

At about noon on Good Friday the gobernador and regional notables gathered near the church. A big jar of tesgüino was brought and the gobernador began serving a small gourdful to each man who stepped forward. This was the official start of the drinking, although some had clearly begun earlier.

Ceremonies like those of the previous day continued until my impressions began to blur, but now for the first time a procession brought the crucifix and the image of the Virgin out of the church and slowly circled the building before returning inside, men carrying the crucifix, women carrying the Virgin. A hint of mourning, perhaps, for the Redeemer.

Toward afternoon the Pharisees and other men, stripped to the breechcloth, painted themselves yellow with clay, getting thoroughly drunk in the process. An official told me in a friendly way that this would be a very good time for Melecio and me to get out. We rode our mules downstream into the dusk, away from the drums and flutes and a hubbub of shouting.

Leaving the Sierra Tarahumara, I thought of a sixtyish, distinguished-looking man from Rejogochi by the name of Basilio. Basilio, agile as a billy goat, would leap around all day long playing *cuatro* — tossing small stone disks into a slightly larger hole — betting lightly and losing steadily to his friend Moreno. They stopped only for the odd drink of pinole. It was neither planting time nor harvest season and little else was to be taken seriously.

I thought of Lupe Nava in his field; of corn ripening to gold; of Felicitas, eagerly returning home; of the last fiesta that helps a soul to heaven; of the reasons any people cherish their own ways above all others.

And I remembered Father Verplancken's words: "The Tarahumaras are no slaves of time or civilization. Why change that? They are always helpful to each other, as they value friendship above material goods; they share corn when needed. I think we really have many things to learn from them. Our job is to help them learn enough that they can take care of themselves when they face the outside world — and can, thereby, keep their own culture, which I consider not lower but different."

With a log loom mounted on rocks, a weaver fashions a multicolored púraca, or sash, in wool from sheep of her flock.

Rumpled canyons and ranges of Chihuahua isolate the Tarahumaras. Scarcity of arable land compels them to farm patches stair-stepped down the canyon walls. Some work plots in the extreme highlands, except when winter's bitter cold sends them migrating to the subtropical climate of the deep canyons. His oxen and his wooden plow a heritage from Spain, an Indian prepares his field for the spring planting of corn. The Tarahumaras cook a large variety of dishes with corn, staple food from time immemorial, by adding other vegetables, fruit, meat on great occasions—and even flowers for seasoning.

Overleaf: In the warm sunlight that Mexicans sometimes call "blanket of the poor," women of Batopilas Canyon prepare food. At right, one grinds roasted corn to powder; a handful mixed into a pint of water becomes pinole, *a standard drink and, says the author, a refreshing one. The woman at left makes* esquiate *much the same way; she adds the water as she grinds the corn.*

Snow arrives in time for Christmas at Ojachichi. Several times a year snow falls on upland Tarahumara country, but seldom stays long on the ground. Wrapped in an extra blanket, but wearing sandals as usual, women venture out. Springtime at Huimaibo softens the landscape's harshness with touches of green. As the morning sun warms the house, a woman herds a flock of goats toward pasture; they have spent the night penned near the house. A woman or child will watch over them during the day. Stone houses with wooden roofs offer minimal shelter from wind and rain. When a family needs a new dwelling, neighbors come to help, requiring about a week to accomplish the task. They bring their own food, knowing that the host will provide tesgüino for them.

*Strong features mirror a strong will. Spanish pressure—
miners seeking slave labor, farmers usurping land and
impressing workers—gradually forced the Indians to retreat
into the rugged country they occupy today. Diseases less easily
escaped, such as tuberculosis, still plague them. The little girl
below is lucky: In nearly inaccessible areas, without medical
services, the infant mortality rate remains extremely high.*

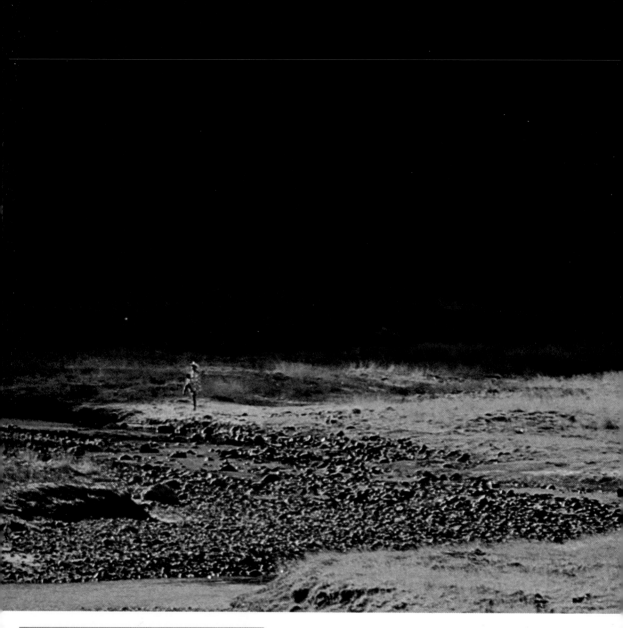

Games of stamina and proofs of skill, developed in tough country, engross the Tarahumaras, who stage notable long-distance races. Men may race for two days and a night, stopping to gulp a few swallows of pinole or esquiate. Above, a sandal-shod runner kicks a small wooden ball along before him. Opposite, men toss a flat rock into a hole to score at cuatro. In the hands of Candelario Martínez (left) a slingshot has a range of some 300 yards. The Indians use this weapon to kill birds or chase coyotes away from their flocks.

In Holy Week, Tarahumara observance colors Catholic ritual—from the manner of blessing to details like feather headdresses. At isolated Munérachi, a procession winds toward the church. No priest came for these services; an Indian goberna-dor delivered a long sermon, exhorting his listeners to give up sin and offering mundane advice on daily affairs. Hour after hour, musicians play homemade drums, violins, and flutes. Feasting and tesgüino-drinking will go on for days. Crosses, prominent in Easter rites, figure in indigenous ceremonies as well; they may represent the four directions, revered in Mexico before the Spanish came.

*For feasting at Eastertide
an oil drum filled with
meat steams over a fire.
Men with wooden rifles or
swords gather at daybreak
to assume the roles of
"soldiers." Above, women
studiously disregard the
gobernador's sermon; and
an owirúame, or shaman,
arrives to join in the ritual.*

206

INDEX

Boldface indicates illustrations;
italic refers to picture captions.

Contributors

Born in Sylvania, Ohio, SAM ABELL received his B.A. in English from the University of Kentucky and taught high-school courses for two years in Toledo. A self-taught photographer, he began his work for the National Geographic Society in 1967 as a summer intern.

A self-described native of the "jungles of Michigan," NAPOLEON A. CHAGNON received his B.A., M.A., and Ph.D. in anthropology from the University of Michigan, now teaches at Pennsylvania State. With Timothy Asch of Brandeis University, he is preparing some 50 ethnographic films on the Yąnomamö.

Born in Lancashire, England, NEVILLE DYSON-HUDSON received his B.A. and M.A. from Cambridge, B. Litt., M.A., and D. Phil. from Oxford. Since 1955 he has studied peoples of eastern Africa. He has taught at the University of Khartoum and at Johns Hopkins, and is now a professor at the State University of New York, Binghamton.

TOR EIGELAND left his native Norway at 16 to go to sea; he studied at McGill University, Mexico City College, and the University of Miami (Florida) before becoming a freelance photojournalist. His recent assignments for the Society include a chapter on Italy for *The Alps.*

Belgian by birth, photojournalist VICTOR ENGLEBERT now lives in New York City. He has traveled extensively in Africa, Asia, and Latin America, contributing to the Society's publications since 1965. He reported on the Tuareg and the Bororo for *Nomads of the World.*

Born in Tecumseh, Michigan, ELMAN R. SERVICE received his B.A. from the University of Michigan and returned there to teach after earning his Ph.D. at Columbia. In 1969 he joined the faculty of the University of California at Santa Barbara. A veteran of extensive fieldwork, he has also published studies of the development of social organization.

E. RICHARD SORENSON received his Ph.D. from Stanford and has traveled or done research in some 65 countries since 1963. His publications encompass theories and methods of anthropology, and research in isolated cultures. He is now engaged in studies of human behavior development at the National Institutes of Health.

A Ph.D. candidate at the University of Chicago, WILSON WHEATCROFT carried out his fieldwork in New Guinea with a research grant from the National Geographic Society. A graduate of the University of Houston, he now teaches at Empire State College in Rochester.

Acknowledgments

The Special Publications Division is grateful to those listed here for their generous cooperation and assistance: Joan Bamberger, David Baradas, Robert A. Bye, Jr., Robert L. Carneiro, J. M. Charpentier, Jean Guiart, Peter B. Hammond, Tom Harrisson, Robert B. Lane, Roque Laraia, David Maybury-Lewis, Pamela Johnson Meyer, Joan Mossman, Kal Muller, W. T. W. Morgan, William Stern, Oscar Trinidad, Terence Turner, Luis J. Verplancken, S.J., Darvall Wilkins; the Australian Baptist Mission, PANAMIN, the Smithsonian Institution.

Additional References

The reader may wish to refer to the following books and to check the *National Geographic Index* for related material: Wendell C. Bennett and Robert M. Zingg, *The Tarahumara;* Napoleon A. Chagnon, *Studying the Yąnomamö, Yąnomamö: the Fierce People,* "Yąnomamö Social Organization and Warfare" in Morton Fried *et al.,* eds., *War: The Anthropology of Armed Conflict and Aggression;* A. Bernard Deacon, *Malekula;* Neville Dyson-Hudson, *Karimojong Politics;* Carlos A. Fernandez and Frank Lynch, S.J., *The Tasaday;* Jean Guiart, *The Arts of the South Pacific;* P. H. Gulliver, *The Family Herds;* Tom Harrisson, *Savage Civilization;* John Layard, *Stone Men of Malekula;* Claude Lévi-Strauss, *The Savage Mind;* Campbell W. Pennington, *The Tarahumar of Mexico;* Kenneth E. Read, *The High Valley;* Marshall D. Sahlins, *Stone Age Economics, The Tribesmen;* Elman R. Service, *The Hunters, Primitive Social Organization, Profiles in Ethnology, Tobati;* Elizabeth Marshall Thomas, *Warrior Herdsmen.*